KU-540-105

WebPlus X4
Resource Guide

Credits

This Resource Guide, and the software described in it, is furnished under an end user License Agreement, which is included with the product. The agreement specifies the permitted and prohibited uses.

Portions images ©1997-2002 Nova Development Corporation; ©1995 Expressions Computer Software; ©1996-98 CreatiCom, Inc.; ©1996 Cliptoart; ©1997 Multimedia Agency Corporation; ©1997-98 Seattle Support Group. Rights of all parties reserved.

Digital Images ©2008 Hemera Technologies Inc. All Rights Reserved.

Digital Images ©2008 Jupiterimages Corporation, All Rights Reserved.

Digital Images ©2008 Jupiterimages France SAS, All Rights Reserved.

Content ©2008 Jupiterimages Corporation. All Rights Reserved.

Portions graphics import/export technology © AccuSoft Corp. &Eastman Kodak Company& LEAD Technologies, Inc.

THE PROXIMITY HYPHENATION SYSTEM © 1989 Proximity Technology Inc. All rights reserved.

THE PROXIMITY/COLLINS DATABASEÒ © 1990 William Collins Sons & Co. Ltd.; © 1990 Proximity Technology Inc. All rights reserved.

THE PROXIMITY/MERRIAM-WEBSTER DATABASEÒ © 1990 Merriam-Webster Inc.; © 1990 Proximity Technology Inc. All rights reserved.

The Sentry Spelling-Checker Engine © 2000 Wintertree Software Inc.

The ThesDB Thesaurus Engine © 1993-97 Wintertree Software Inc.

WGrammar Grammar-Checker Engine © 1998 Wintertree Software Inc.

Andrei Stcherbatchenko, Ferdinand Prantl

eBay © 1995-2008 eBay Inc. All Rights Reserved.

PayPal © 1999-2008 PayPal. All rights reserved.

Roman Cart © 2008 Roman Interactive Ltd. All rights reserved.

Mal's © 1998 to 2003 Mal's e-commerce Ltd. All rights reserved.

iTunes © 2000 to 2008 Apple Computer, Inc. All rights reserved.

YouTube © 2008 YouTube, LLC

phpBB © 2000, 2002, 2003, 2007 phpBB Group

FontForge © 2000,2001,2002,2003,2004,2005,2006,2007,2008 by George Williams.

Portions of this software are copyright © 2008 The FreeType Project (www.freetype.org). All rights reserved.

ODF Translator © 2006-2008, Clever Age, DIaLOGIKa, Sonata Software Ltd. All rights reserved.

Office Binary Translator to OpenXML Copyright © 2008-2009, DIaLOGIKa. All rights reserved.

Anti-Grain Geometry - Version 2.4

Copyright © 2002-2005 Maxim Shemanarev (McSeem)

SlideShowPro © Dominey Design Inc. All rights reserved.

Clipart samples from Serif ArtPacks © Serif (Europe) Ltd. & Paul Harris

TrueType font samples from Serif FontPacks © Serif (Europe) Ltd.

Microsoft, Windows, and the Windows logo are registered trademarks of Microsoft Corporation. All other trademarks acknowledged.

WebPlus is a registered trademark of Serif (Europe) Ltd.

© 2009 Serif (Europe) Ltd. All rights reserved. No part of this Resource Guide may be reproduced in any form without the express written permission of Serif (Europe) Ltd.

Serif WebPlus X4 © 2009 Serif (Europe) Ltd.

Contacting Serif

Contacting Serif technical support

Our support mission is to provide fast, friendly technical advice and support from a team of on-call experts. Technical support is provided from our web support page, and useful information can be obtained via our web-based forums (see below). There are no pricing policies after the 30 day money back guarantee period.

UK/International/
US Technical Support :   **http://www.serif.com/support**

Additional Serif contact information

Web:

Serif website: **http://www.serif.com**

Forums: **http://www.serif.com/forums.asp**

Main office (UK, Europe):

The Software Centre, PO Box 2000, Nottingham, NG11 7GW, UK

Main: (0115) 914 2000

Registration (UK only):   (0800) 376 1989

Sales (UK only):   (0800) 376 7070

Customer Service
(UK/International):   **http://www.serif.com/support**

General Fax: (0115) 914 2020

North American office (US, Canada):

The Software Center, 13 Columbia Drive, Suite 5, Amherst NH 03031, USA

Main: (603) 889-8650

Registration: (800) 794-6876

Sales: (800) 55-SERIF or 557-3743

Customer Service: **http://www.serif.com/support**

General Fax: (603) 889-1127

International enquiries

Please contact our main office.

Contents

Introduction

Whether you are new to WebPlus or a seasoned website designer, the Resource Guide offers content to help you get the best out of WebPlus.

From a range of novice and professional tutorials to get you started or help you accomplish a complex project, to full-colour previews of the design templates, theme layouts, and navigation bars, the Resource Guide is something you'll return to time and time again.

The Resource Guide is organized into the following chapters:

- **Chapter 1: Tutorials**—Illustrated, step-by-step training covering the basics of WebPlus and website design, along with some more challenging projects.

- **Chapter 2: Theme Layouts**
  Full-colour page previews of the theme layouts included on the WebePlus X4 Program CD.

- **Chapter 3: Navigation Bars**
  Previews of the customizable JavaScript and Flash™ navigation bars included with WebPlus, and instructions on how to add them to your sites.

- **Chapter 4: Templates**
  A reference gallery of the design templates available on the WebPlus X4 Program CD and its accompanying Resource CD.

Tutorials

Introduction

The tutorials provide step-by-step instructions to help you get the most out of WebPlus, and guide you through the process of creating professional-looking and effective websites. The tutorials are grouped into the following categories:

Getting Started

Aimed at the new user, these exercises introduce the WebPlus user interface and the key tools and features required to create a website.

Dynamic Content

Aimed at both beginners and more experienced WebPlus users, these tutorials show you how to add dynamic content to your site.

Topics covered include Flash™ photo galleries and banners, as well as a selection of the smart objects hosted by Serif Web Resources.

Further Development

This section provides more advanced exercises to help you develop your site by including e-commerce functionality, iFrames, HTML code fragments, and database-merged fields.

> The tutorials are also presented as PDF files, which you can print out or view on screen.
>
> If viewing on screen, you can quickly switch between WebPlus and the tutorial document by pressing the **Alt + Tab** keys.

Getting Started

Aimed at the new user, these exercises introduce the
WebPlus user interface and the key tools and features
required to create a website.

Site Structure

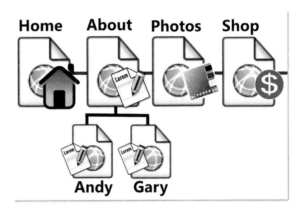

WebPlus provides simple, powerful tools that make it easy to design clearly structured websites that are easy to navigate. In this tutorial, we'll use a WebPlus template to introduce you to the basic elements of site structure. You'll familiarize yourself with the WebPlus workspace, and learn how to:

- Make adjustments to and preview a site.
- View site structure.
- Add and rearrange pages.

Site Structure

WebPlus lets you assemble all the elements of your site-in-progress into one multi-page document that can be saved as a WebPlus project file.

Creating a website in WebPlus can be as simple as choosing and customizing a design template, a theme layout, or you can start from scratch.

We'll introduce a typical site structure by working with a WebPlus template.

A website is basically a collection of separate pages with hyperlinks connecting them. Any visitor who enters your site will need help getting around. As the 'architect' of this entity, it's your job to arrange your content in a logical and accessible way, and provide navigational signposts that quickly convey how the site is organized.

To open a WebPlus template

1   From the **StartUp Wizard** choose **Use Design Template**.

2   Navigate to the **Interest** category and select the **Reactive** template.

3   Click **Open**.

The template site opens with the **Home** page displayed in the workspace. This is a simple site with just eight pages; at the right of the workspace you'll see them listed on the **Site** tab.

To view your site

1   On the toolbar at the top of the workspace, click the arrow on the ▢ ▾ **Preview Site** button to expand a list of preview options.

2   Select **Preview Site in {browser of choice}**. WebPlus generates the necessary temporary files and opens a new browser window displaying the site's Home page.

At the top of the page you'll see a **navigation bar** (sometimes shortened to navbar) consisting of five buttons. Click the buttons to navigate quickly between the five 'top-level' pages of the site.

Home	Facilities	Fitness	Bookings	Contact Us

The navigation bar interconnects the site's pages and is an indispensable element of site design. Users will expect it to be there, they'll know what to do with it, and it will help them grasp your site's main content sections at a glance.

Once you've experimented with the navigation bar, close the browser window and return to WebPlus.

To save your work

1 Before proceeding, click **File**, then **Save As...**

2 Save your project file with a file name of your choice. Note that saving the WebPlus (.wpp) project file is not the same as publishing it as a website.

Understanding site structure

Let's take a few moments to examine the site we created from the template.

The WebPlus workspace consists of:

- A **page area**, where you put the text, graphics, and other elements you want to appear on the final Web page.

- A surrounding pasteboard area, where you can keep elements that are being prepared or waiting to be positioned on the page area.

- Horizontal and vertical **toolbars** and **tabs**, used to access WebPlus commands and tools.

Move the mouse pointer around the screen and you'll see popup **tooltips** that identify toolbar buttons and flyouts.

Right-click any object or page region to bring up a **context menu** of functions... the choices probably seem overwhelming at this point!

The **Hintline** toolbar at the bottom of the workspace provides context-sensitive information and tips about selected objects, buttons, and menu items.

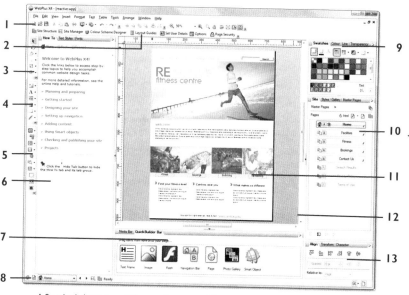

1 Standard, Arrange and View toolbars
2 Context toolbars
3 Tools toolbar
4 Standard Objects toolbar
5 Web Objects toolbar
6 How To, Text Styles, & Fonts tabs
7 Media Bar and QuickBuilder Bar

8 Page Locator and Hintline toolbar
9 Swatches, Colour, Line, Transparency tabs
10 Site, Style, Gallery, Master Pages tabs
11 Page area
12 Pasteboard area
13 Align, Transform, Character tabs

Let's now look at some different ways to get an overview of the entire site.

To navigate between pages

1 At the right of the workspace, click the **Site** tab. This tab displays the **Site Structure tree** for this particular site. You'll recognize the entries as the main pages of the site.

2 Double-click a page entry to open it in the workspace.

As you change pages, notice that the icon moves to indicate which page is currently in view and ready for editing.

3   In the lower left corner of the workspace, the

🏠 Home ▼ **Page Locator** button shows the name of the current page. Click the button to display a list of the site's pages.

4   This time, single-click any page entry to view it.

Watch the **Site** tab and you'll see the ☉ icon indicating the page on view.

5   If you single-click on a page in the tab, the page entry changes colour but the page is not displayed in the workspace. However, you can edit page properties and update other details.

💡 **When using the Site tab:**

• Single-click a page to select it—which you might do, for example, if you wanted to delete the page, or change its properties.

• Double-click a page to view it or edit its design elements.

🔖 The vertical order of the Web pages corresponds to the order in which they appear in the navigation bar. Page entries are connected by dotted lines, implying a certain relatedness.

To insert a child page

1   On the **Site** tab, right-click the entry for the **Contact Us** page, and choose **Insert Page...**

2   In the **New Page Properties** dialog:

• On the **Navigation** tab, in the **Page name:** text box, type 'Joe'.

• Change the **File name:** to 'joe.html'.

• On the **Appearance** tab, in the **Placement** section, select the **Child of:** option.

• Click **OK**.

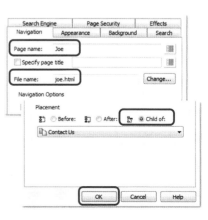

Web page hierarchy

Having inserted a new page in the 'Contact Us' section of the site, we now have the makings of a hierarchy. Now the dotted lines connecting the page entries make more sense, and the Site Structure tree is no longer just a list.

You can see how this parent-and-child 'tree' structure provides a natural framework for organizing site content into sections and levels. In this site, we've begun with one main page at the top level for each of our main sections: Home, Fitness, Facilities, Bookings and Contact Us. Over time we would expect to add subsidiary (child) pages to each section, at lower levels.

A new page opens in the workspace, along with a new entry on the **Site** tab—which tells us the page title is 'Joe' and that it's currently on view (note the 👁 icon) but not selected (the **Contact Us** page is).

More importantly, notice that the new 'Joe' page entry is indented under **Contact Us**—in other words it's a child of **Contact Us**, just as we specified in the dialog.

Navigating pages

There are times when you don't want a page to appear in your site navigation. This is easy to achieve in WebPlus.

On the **Site** tab, pages that are not included in the navigation are a different colour, and do not have a red check mark next to their names.

To change navigation options

1   On the **Site** tab, right-click the **Facilities** page entry and click **Page Properties...**

2   In the **Page Properties** dialog, in the **Navigation** tab, clear the **Include in Navigation** check box and then click **OK**.

Notice what happens in the navigation bar: Switching off the **Include in Navigation** setting for a page forces navigation bars to ignore that page, and its button disappears.

3 Click on another page on the **Site** tab.

Now take a look at the **page list**. Notice that the **Facilities** entry has changed colour and its red check mark is no longer displayed.

4 Open the **Page Properties** dialog again and select the **Include in Navigation** check box to reset it.

Page order

The buttons at the bottom of the **Site** tab also allow you to quickly and easily change pages from child to parent, or to move pages up or down in the list. To use any of these buttons, select the page that you want to move and then click the relevant button.

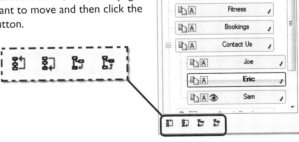

To change page order

1 On the **Site** tab, click to select the **Contact Us** page.

2 Click the **Move Page Up** button.

The page moves up the list while staying at the same hierarchy.

Notice that the child pages are also moved as they are dependent on the parent page.

The navigation bar updates automatically to mirror the new top-level page order.

3 Experiment with the other pages and buttons.

Because most people grasp a branching structure fairly quickly, organizing your content into a 'tree' structure helps your visitor navigate through it. As we've seen in this tutorial, the **Site** tab serves as a control centre that lets you, the designer, not only visualize your site's framework but manipulate it with ease.

You should now understand a little about site structure and how navigation bars adapt instantly to changes in the structure.

💡 Drag and Drop

You can change the order of the pages in the **Site** tab by dragging page entries to a different position.

Watch the cursor change when you drag:

- indicates that you can make the dropped page a child of the page above.

- indicates that the page will land on the same level.

Text

A website is only ever as good as its content, and chances are, a lot of that content is made up of text. In this tutorial we'll introduce you to the different types of text available for you to use in WebPlus.

In this exercise, we'll discuss the details surrounding the creation and editing of text.

- Create and edit Artistic text and HTML text frames.
- Learn about Text Styles and HTML meta tags.

Text

There are three types of text that you can use in WebPlus—Artistic text, HTML Frame text and Creative Frame text. You can use the same methods to perform operations such as selecting, editing, and formatting all types of text. However, there are a few important differences, as outlined in the following quick-reference table:

Artistic text:
- Standalone text that can be typed directly onto a page.
- Stretch or squash the text to create a stylistic effect.
- Create shaped text by putting the text on a path.
- Apply instant 3D effects.
- Is especially useful for titles, pull quotes, and other special-purpose text.
- Not searchable by search engines.
- May be published as text or as an image, depending on the formatting applied.

HTML Frame text:
- Placed on the page inside a *text frame*,
- Is generally used for longer passages of text, or non-decorative text such as contact details, product information, etc.
- The frame can be resized without altering the text properties.
- Published with true HTML paragraph tags (H1, H2, P etc.).
- Searchable by search engines such as Google™.
- Always published as text.

Creative Frame text:
- Generally used for longer passages of special-purpose text.
- Lets you flow text between multiple text frames.
- Allows you to apply some special effects and formatting.
- Not searchable by search engines.
- May be published as text or as an image, depending on the formatting applied.

Artistic Text

Many of the methods used to edit text in WebPlus are the same regardless of text type. We'll show you most of these by introducing our first text type, *artistic text*. Let's open a new site project.

To open a new site

- From the WebPlus Startup Wizard, click **Start New Site**.

Now let's create a nameplate for a fictitious diving club, the Scuba Sharks. For this, we'll use artistic text...

To create artistic text

1   On the Standard Objects toolbar, on the A ˅ Text flyout, click the A **Artistic Text Tool**.

2   Click anywhere on your page to set a text insertion point.

3   On the Text context toolbar, in the Fonts drop-down list, select a bold font. We used Arial Black.

4   Type 'SCUBA'.

5   In the lower-left corner of the workspace, the HintLine toolbar tells us that this is Artistic Text.

Now that our first word is placed, let's make it a little more interesting.

To accurately resize artistic text

1   With the text object still selected, on the **Transform** tab, ensure that the **Lock Aspect Ratio** is off. (If not, click the button once.)

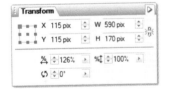

2   Change the Width to **590 pix** and then change the Height to **170 pix**.

3   Click and drag the ✛ **Move** button located just above the upper-left corner of the object (or click and drag on the object's border) to drag the object into position as illustrated.

We can make the artistic text more interesting by adding a gradient fill.

To apply a gradient fill

1   With the text still selected, go to the **Swatches** tab.

2   Expand the ▣· **Gradient Fills** flyout and select **Linear**.

3   Click the **Linear Fill 14** swatch to apply it to the text.

The gradient colour spread works well, but we can change the gradient to use scheme colours. This means that if we use the text in another document, it will tie in with any colour scheme.

To edit a gradient fill

1   Select the text object and then on the Tools toolbar, click the ◇ **Fill Tool**.

    The object's fill path is displayed.

2   On the Fill context toolbar:

    • In the **Fill Start** drop-down list, select swatch 7 on the Scheme 5 row.

    • In the **Fill End** drop-down list, select swatch 5 on the Scheme 2 row.

3   (Optional) You can also adjust the fill path by clicking and dragging the fill path nodes.

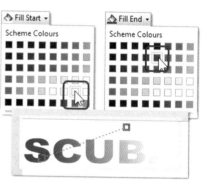

The first part of our title is almost complete; however, let's make it look really special by adding a reflection effect.

To apply a reflection effect

1   With the text object selected, go to the **Styles** tab and in the categories drop-down list, select **Reflection**.

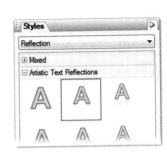

2   In the **Artistic Text Reflections** sub-category, click the **Text Reflection 02 : FilterEffects** preset.

The reflection is applied.

To edit a reflection effect

1   With the text object selected, on the Tools toolbar, in the **Effects** flyout, click the *fx* **Filter Effects** button.

2   In the dialog:

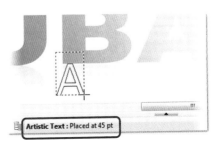

- If the preview is displayed, click ▷ **Show/Hide Preview** to hide the preview.

    - Drag the **Offset** slider to the left until the reflection sits just below the text. (The effect previews on the page.)

    - Click **OK**. The reflection is updated.

Next, we'll add our second word of our club name, 'SHARKS'. This time, we'll use another Artistic text object but we'll apply an **Instant 3D** style.

To create 3D text

1   On the Tools toolbar, on the A ▾ Text flyout, click the A **Artistic Text Tool**.

2   Click and drag anywhere on your page to create a text insertion point approximately 45 pt.

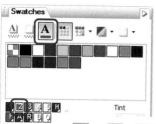

3 On the Text context toolbar, change the font to the same one as before, e.g. Arial Black.

4 On the **Swatches** tab, click the **A** **Text** button and then click the **Scheme Colour 2** swatch.

5 Type 'SHARKS'.

6 With the text object still selected, go to the **Styles** tab, and in the categories drop-down list, click **3D**.

7 In the **Mixed** sub-category, click the **3D 06 : Warp** preset.

The effect is applied.

8 On the **Transform** tab, rotate the objects by -9°.

- or -

Hover next to a corner handle and use the rotate cursor to rotate the object.

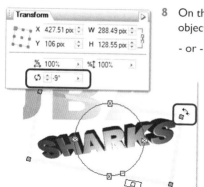

To edit the text in an instant 3D object, select the object and click [▢]. The text displays with a coloured outline. To select all of the text, press **Ctrl + A**; to select a word or range of text, click and drag. You can now format the text style, font, size, colour etc. in the usual way.

For more information about Instant 3D, see the topic *Adding dimensionality (Instant 3D)* in online Help.

9 Finally, click and drag the ✛ **Move** button to drag the object into position as illustrated.

Now that we've created the club nameplate, we can add it to the gallery for use in other projects.

To add objects to the Gallery

1 Place the pointer in the workspace and then click and drag to select both objects with a selection marquee.

2 Click the ▦ **Group** button.

3 On the **Gallery** tab, in the category drop-down list, select **My Designs**.

4 Press and hold the **Ctrl** key and drag a copy of the nameplate onto the **Gallery** tab.

5 In the dialog, type 'ScubaSharks' and click **OK**.

A copy of the object appears in the tab and is now ready for use in all of your future projects!

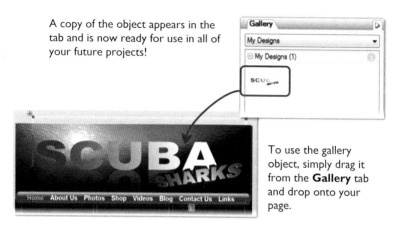

To use the gallery object, simply drag it from the **Gallery** tab and drop onto your page.

You'll see from the illustration above that the text colour looks different from our original design. This is because the document had a different colour scheme. When we applied the gradient fill, we used scheme colours. This means that the text will always use the current colour scheme. See the *Colour Schemes* tutorial or online Help for more information.

Now that we've looked at Artistic text, let's have a look at another important text type—*HTML frame text*.

HTML frame text

Any time you add effects such as bitmap fills, transparency, and filter effects to an artistic text object, the object is converted to a graphic when it is published. Similarly, in a Creative text frame, if you use an unusual font, or apply special formatting, the text will instead be rendered as a graphic. This can increase the download time of your website, and prevent the use of screen readers.

To make your site as accessible as possible to everyone, you should use HTML text frames for your content. Let's start a new site so that we have a blank canvas.

To open a new site

- On the Standard toolbar, click 🗋 **New Site** and then, from the WebPlus Startup Wizard, click **Start New Site**.

To place an HTML text frame

1 On the Standard Objects toolbar, in the ▣ ▾ Text Frame flyout, click the ▣ **HTML Frame Tool**.

2 Click and drag on the page to insert the frame at a size of your choice.

- or -

Click once on the page to insert the frame at its default size.

The HintLine toolbar tells you that this is an *HTML frame*.

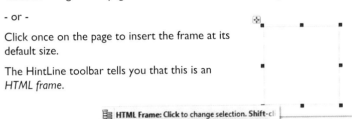

🗐 HTML Frame: Click to change selection. Shift-cl

Let's now fill our frame with some text. To save time when designing a site, you can fill any text frame (Creative or HTML) with placeholder text. This can help you (or your client) to visualise the overall design before the actual content is added.

Welcome

Vestibulum velit orci, bibendum eget, molestie eu, sagittis non, leo. Nullam sed enim. Duis ac orem. Lorem ipsum dolor sit amet, consectetuer adipiscing elit. Suspendisse potenti. Sed

To create placeholder text

1 Click inside the text frame to create an insertion point, and then type the word 'Welcome'. Press **Enter** to drop to the next line.

2 On the **Insert** menu, click **Fill with Placeholder Text**.

To select, edit and format text

1 Click to place an insertion point after the word 'Welcome' and press the Spacebar. Type 'to ScubaSharks!'.

2 Triple-click (or click and drag) on the first line of text to select it.

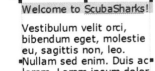

Welcome to ScubaSharks!

Vestibulum velit orci, bibendum eget, molestie eu, sagittis non, leo. Nullam sed enim. Duis ac lorem. Lorem ipsum dolor sit amet, consectetuer adipiscing elit. Suspendisse potenti. Sed

3   On the Text context toolbar, in the styles drop-down list, select
    Heading 1.

    The heading is updated.

If you placed the frame at its default size
as we have done, you might find that the
text no longer fits. You may also see an
☐ Overflow button. This means that
there is more text in the frame than can
fit at one time. However, it's easy to
resize a frame without changing the
appearance of the text within. Let's do
this now.

To resize a frame by dragging

1   Move the mouser pointer over the frame's right-centre
    handle. The pointer will change to a double-headed arrow.

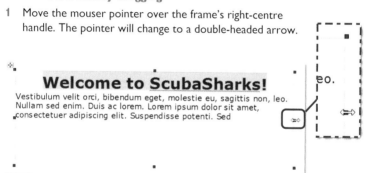

2   Click and drag to the right until the heading fits in the frame.

    The text formatting doesn't change, it simply re-aligns to fit within the
    boundaries of the frame.

When you resize an HTML or Creative text frame, you are
only resizing the text *container*. The formatting of the text will
not change. However, resizing an Artistic text object once it is
placed on the page will change the formatting of the text itself.
Artistic text that is stretched or squashed will always be output
as a graphic.

Let's add another heading to our text frame. This time, we'll format it using the **Heading 2** text style.

To format text using text styles

1   Click inside the text frame to create an insertion point, and then press **Enter** to drop to the next line. Type the words 'PADI Scuba courses'.

2   On the Text context toolbar, in the styles drop-down list, select **Heading 2**.

    The style is applied to the text.

To select, copy and paste text

1   Triple-click on the paragraph in the text frame. The entire paragraph is selected.

2   On the Standard toolbar, click 📋 **Copy** (or press **Ctrl + C**).

3   Click next to the word 'courses' and press **Enter** to create a new line.

4   Click 📋 **Paste** (or press **Ctrl + V**). The text is inserted.

Welcome to ScubaSharks!

Vestibulum velit orci, bibendum eget, molestie eu, sagittis non, leo.
Nullam sed enim. Duis ac lorem. Lorem ipsum dolor sit amet,
consectetuer adipiscing elit. Suspendisse potenti. Sed

PADI Scuba courses

Vestibulum velit orci, bibendum eget, molestie eu, sagittis non, leo.
Nullam sed enim. Duis ac lorem. Lorem ipsum dolor sit amet,
consectetuer adipiscing elit. Suspendisse potenti. Sed

💡 **Changing the font**

You can choose any font you like for your HTML text.

However, unless you are certain that your site visitors have a particular 'non-Websafe' font installed on their computers, we recommend that you select from the Websafe list for best possible results.

Although 'non-Websafe' text will not be converted to a graphic, you have no way of knowing how it will appear onscreen to site visitors.

Text Styles

By using text styles, it makes it easy to keep the formatting of your text consistent. By default, each style is based on the **Normal** text style, so, by modifying Normal, the change is reflected throughout all of the Text Styles (and therefore your site). This makes it easy to quickly change the font, size and colour of your entire site.

We'll illustrate this by changing the text colour.

To update a text style

1   Click or hover over the ⬩ handle (near the Web Objects toolbar) to open the **Text Styles** tab.

2   Move the mouse pointer over the **Normal** style and click the down-arrow. (If the Normal style is not displayed, check **Show All** at the bottom of the Text Styles tab.)

3   Click **Modify Normal...**

4   In the **Text Style** dialog:

- In the left pane, in the **Character** category, click the **Font** sub-category.

- Click to expand the **Text colour** drop-down list and then click the Scheme Colour 2 swatch.

- Click **OK**.

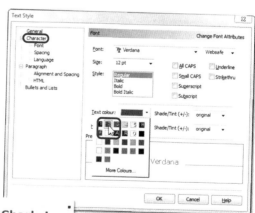

All of the text in the frame is updated with the new colour!

We couldn't finish this tutorial without looking at the main advantage of using HTML text frames—HTML meta tags. These are used by search engines to categorize your site. If you assign a meta tag to a text style, WebPlus will automatically generate the code when the site is published.

The **Text Styles** tab contains preset Heading styles which translate to HTML tags H1 to H6. You can format the text style to suit your site design whilst keeping those important tags. For more information on modifying text styles see online Help.

Let's do this now.

To apply an HTML meta tag to a style

1   On the **Text Styles** tab, move the mouse pointer over the **Heading 1** style and click the down-arrow.

2   Click **Modify Heading 1...**

3   In the **Text Style** dialog:

    • In the left pane, in the **Paragraph** category, click the **HTML** sub-category.

    • Select the appropriate HTML tag (in this case H1 is already selected).

    • Click **OK**.

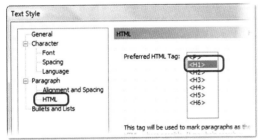

The H1 tag will be applied whenever the **Heading 1** style is used within an HTML text frame.

Creative text frames

Creative text frames are a cross between Artistic text and HTML frame text. They are especially useful for pull quotes and other text where special formatting is needed. However, this special functionality means that they are not compliant with web standards and cannot be searched by search engines. As such, we recommend that they are either used for internal sites or only used for short passages and pull-quotes. For more information on creating and publishing text and text frames, see *Understanding text frames* in online Help

When you publish your website, any text that uses a non-solid fill, a line style other than **None**, a filter effect, a 3D effect, transparency, or horizontal or vertical resizing will be output as a **graphic** (which makes your pages load more slowly compared to using plain text). Artistic text that does not have these effects applied will be output as **text**.

For more information, see the *Web-Friendly Sites* PDF tutorial, available from the Learning Zone.

We've covered many useful tips for creating, editing, and managing text with WebPlus. We hope that you're now feeling more comfortable with the different text objects we've described and are ready to get started creating content for your own site!

Hyperlinks

MY LINKS

RUN4CHARITY
JACKDAW'S ORGANIC FARM
ORGANIC FOOD TO GO
SLOPES & SKIS

WebPlus provides a wide and very flexible range of hyperlink options. This means easy navigation for your site's visitors— and possibly a more efficient visit if your site includes large pictures.

In this exercise, you'll learn how to:

- Create text objects and import pictures.
- Create anchors.
- Create and edit hyperlinks.
- Create self-linking picture hyperlinks.

Creating Hyperlinks and Anchors

In this tutorial, we'll explore the various hyperlink options and demonstrate a couple of useful WebPlus features.

To create the anchors

1   From the Startup Wizard, choose **Create > Start New Site** (or click **File**, and then click **New**).

Our project has one page and no content—we'll add some content to demonstrate the use of hyperlinks, but we won't build a full site.

2   Select the Λ **Artistic Text Tool** and drag the mouse cursor until the text size is approximately 50 points— as you drag, watch the Hintline to see the text size.

Artistic Text : Placed at 50.25 pt

3   Write a title for your page and place the text near the upper-middle section of your page.

4   Create another text object, approximately 24 pt text size, on the left of the page and type 'Section 1'.

WebPlus

Section 1
Section 2
Section 3
Section 4

Section 1
Section 2
Section 3
Section 4

5   Hold down the **Ctrl** key, then click and drag on the border of the text object. On release, a copy of the object is dropped on your page. Repeat twice to create a total of four text objects.

6   Edit the text objects so that they read Section 1, Section 2, Section 3, and Section 4.

7   Click and drag on the page to create a selection across the objects.

8   On the **Align** tab:

- Ensure that **Relative to:** is set to **Selection**.

- Click ⌈⌐ **Align Left**.

- Select the **Spaced** option and set the spacing to **120pt**.

- Click 😓 **Space Evenly Down**.

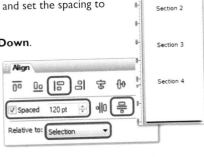

9   Select the **Section 1** text object. On the Tools toolbar, click to expand the 🔒 ▾ **Hyperlink** flyout and then click the ⚓ **Anchor** button.

In the **Anchor** dialog box, type 'Section1,' and then click **OK**. (Note that anchor names cannot contain spaces.)

We've just added an 'anchor' to one of our objects. But what does it do? Simply put, it's like placing a bookmark in a book; it defines a place you can jump to quickly.

However, an anchor doesn't just take you to a certain page like a bookmark does, it allows a hyperlink to take you to a specific point on a web page!

💡 Anchors can be added to any object on any page, so it's possible to create unique navigation, and to offer speedy access to your site's content.

Anchors for important parts of your site can be included within site navigation maps or navigation bars by checking the **Include Anchor In Navigation** option. (Make sure that you give the anchor a meaningful title as this is what your site visitors will see.)

10 Repeat the previous step for each of your text objects, naming the anchors to correspond with the section names.

Let's create the objects that we are going to hyperlink from...

To create the hyperlinks

1   Select the Λ **Artistic Text Tool** and click once on the page to create a text object with default settings. Type 'Section 1' again.

2   Create copies of the object as described in step 5 of the previous section. Edit the text objects to match the section headers created earlier.

3   Position the text objects in a row under your title text and then select them all by dragging a selection bounding box around them.

WebPlus

Section 1   Section 2   Section 3   Section 4

Section 1

On the **Align** tab:

Align

Relative to: Selection

Spaced   120 pt

• Ensure that **Relative to:** is set to **Selection**.

• Click ⟨⟩ **Centre Vertically**.

• Clear the **Spaced** option and click ⊪ **Space Evenly Across**.

4   Click on the small **Section 1** text object near the top of your page to select it.

Click on the grey border of the object to select it as a whole—if there is a flashing 'text-edit' cursor then your hyperlink will not link from the entire line of text.

5   Click the arrow next to the ↕ **Anchor** tool to display the Hyperlink flyout again, then click the ◉ **Hyperlink** tool.

6   In the **Hyperlinks** dialog:

- Select **Anchor**.

- All of your site's anchors are listed in the **Anchor** drop-down list. Choose the anchor called **Section1**.

- In the **Title** text box, type 'Jump to Section 1'.

- Click **OK**.

 The **Export as absolute URL** option lets your site visitors add your page as a bookmark. This is especially important if you use frames to display content within your site.

7   Repeat the previous step to add hyperlinks between the remaining small text objects and section heading anchors.

8   Click the ⬛▾ **Preview Site** button to see how your hyperlinks and anchors work when the page is published and viewed in a web browser.

Notice that the titles you typed display when you hover the cursor over a hyperlink.

Close your browser when you have explored your new links.

Long web pages

For long web pages with anchors towards the bottom of the page you may want to also offer a link back to the top of the page, often just called 'Top.' You don't need to use an anchor to do this. In the following steps we'll show you how.

To create a 'top' link

1   Create a text object, type the word 'Top' and position it at the lower edge of the page. This will serve as our 'button.'

2 Select the object's border, and click the
   🐾 **Hyperlink** tool to add a hyperlink.

3 In the **Hyperlinks** dialog:

   • Select **Anchor**.

   • In the
     Anchor
     drop-down
     list, click **top**.

   • Click **OK**.

4 Preview your
   site to test this
   link.

Linking to pictures

We've just examined how to jump to specific points on a page, but
hyperlinks can perform other tasks too. In the next section, we show you
how to link to a larger version of a picture.

To create a 'self-linking' picture

1 Click the 🖼 **Import Picture** button.

2 In the **Import Picture** dialog, browse to your own pictures folder.

   • Select an image file.

   • Select the **Link Picture** option and click **Open**.

Back in the workspace, note that your cursor has changed to the Picture Import cursor. You can single-click to import the picture at its original size, or click and drag to set the size of the picture.

3 Click just under the **Section 1** heading at the left of the page and drag until the height of the picture spans half the distance between the **Section 1** and **Section 2** headings.

Release the mouse when you are happy with the image size.

4 With the image selected, press **Ctrl+K** to open the **Hyperlinks** dialog.

In the **Hyperlinks** dialog:

- Choose the **Picture** option.

- In the
  Target
  Window or
  Frame
  drop-down
  list, choose
  New
  Window.

- Click **OK**.

5 Preview your site in a browser of your choice to see this hyperlink option in action, clicking on the picture thumbnail to link to the full-size image.

💡 You can set image **Title** options—text that appears when you hover over the image— within the **Image Export Options** dialog. For more information, see the *Pictures* tutorial.

You can use this 'self-linking picture' hyperlink method to build an online image gallery displaying thumbnails that viewers can click on to view the full size image.

6   Go back to your project, right-click the small image and choose **Properties.** You'll see that the thumbnail image is much smaller then the original image (in our case, 95 x 142 pixels).

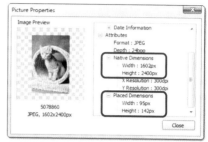

When our site was published to a temporary folder for previewing purposes, WebPlus noticed that our resized 'thumbnail' was much smaller than the original image, so it created a much smaller version to make our page download more quickly. The original 1602 x 2400 pixel image was 512950 bytes. However, because WebPlus has resized the thumbnail, the image that loads with the page is only 101515 bytes. This is far more efficient and makes for a much faster page load!

We'll leave you to explore the other hyperlink types—they are more self-explanatory in their nature, linking to other Web addresses, email addresses, other pages in your site, and so on.

Hyperlinks and anchors can be viewed and managed from the Site **Manager**, which you can access from the context toolbar.

For more information on using **Site Manager**, see online Help.

Pictures

In this tutorial, we'll introduce you to importing, placing, and managing images on your website. Along the way, we'll also highlight some useful dos and don'ts.

In this exercise, you will:

- Import and place images on the page.
- Create self-linking picture hyperlinks.
- Learn about image resolution and resizing.
- Apply various image effects.
- Use picture frames.
- Learn how to use ALT and TITLE text.

Placing and optimizing pictures

Using pictures is a great way to create an eye-catching website. However, used incorrectly, they can cause your site to be slow to load. WebPlus has a few tricks up its sleeve to help you place your images and optimize your page download. In the first section of this tutorial we'll help you to avoid this common pitfall, and optimize your page download time.

To place an image on the page

1   From the Startup Wizard, choose **Create > Start New Site**, or on the **File** menu, click **New**.

2   On the Tools toolbar, click 🖼 **Import Picture**.

In the **Import Picture** dialog:

• Browse to the **Workspace** folder. In a default installation, you'll find this in the following location:

C:\Program Files\Serif\WebPlus\X4\Tutorials

• Select the **MG.jpg** file and then click **Open**.

Your cursor changes to the 🖼 Picture Import cursor.

Single-click on your page to import the image at its native size.

3   Repeat step 2, but instead, click and drag on the page to create a small 'thumbnail' version of the image.

💡 You can also scale an image at any time by selecting it and dragging its handles.

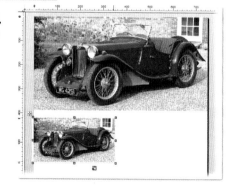

To preview published image size

1   On the Standard toolbar, click to expand the 🖵 ▾ **Preview Site** drop-down list and click **Preview in Window**.

2   Right-click each image in turn and click **Image Properties**.

Notice that the smaller image also has a smaller file size. (Note also that the files are no longer called **MG.jpg**. This is because WebPlus has created new versions of the image.)

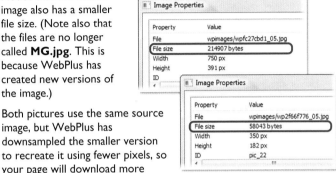

Both pictures use the same source image, but WebPlus has downsampled the smaller version to recreate it using fewer pixels, so your page will download more quickly.

3   Click ⊠ **Close Preview** to return to the WebPlus workspace.

Upsampling and downsampling

The terms **downsampling** and **upsampling** are used to describe the recreation of images with either fewer or more pixels respectively.

An upsampled image has more pixels than the original, and can be done in image editing software such as **Serif PhotoPlus**. The additional pixels are added by clever mathematical guesswork. Upsampled images often have a larger file size than the original image.

A downsampled image has fewer pixels than the original, and therefore, a smaller file size. When an image has been reduced in size on the page, WebPlus generally downsamples automatically at publication time, outputting a reduced-resolution image that fits the space allocated to it on the page.

Suppose you want your site's visitors to be able to view high-resolution images while keeping the page size small. Here's an excellent approach:

To create a self-linking hyperlink

1   Click on the large image to select it and then press **Delete**.

2   Select the small image and reposition it towards the top of the page.

3   With the image still selected, on the Tools toolbar, click 🖳 **Hyperlink**.

4   In the **Hyperlinks** dialog, select the **Picture** option and click **OK**.

5   In the 🖳 ▾ **HTML Preview** drop-down list, click **Preview in {your Web browser of choice}**.

Hover the mouse over the image—the cursor changes to a hand. Click to see a full-size version of the image.

6   Close the browser preview when you have finished experimenting.

This 'self-linking picture' hyperlink method is a favoured way of offering images to your site's visitors—the smaller image is quick to download, providing faster-loading pages, and only the visitors who want to see the full size image need to download it. This eliminates unnecessary bandwidth usage.

Applying adjustments and effects

Now let's move on and discuss a few more hints and tips for enhancing your pictures...

To add transparency effects

1   With the image selected, click the **Transparency** tab and expand the ⌐ ▾ **Bitmap** drop-down list.

2   Click to display the **Photo Edge Effects** category and then click the **Bitmap Transparency 10** swatch.

3 Click to expand the 🖥 ▾ **HTML Preview** drop-down list and click **Preview in Window**.

Let's now see how these changes have affected the way in which WebPlus publishes the image.

4 In your browser, right-click on the image and choose **Properties**.

Note the image size (53817 bytes in our case). This is different to the reported size of our original thumbnail image, placed in step 2 (58043 bytes).

Property	Value
File	wpimages/wp348a3b13_05.jpg
File size	53817 bytes
Width	350 px
Height	182 px
ID	pic_22

The use of transparency on our image means that WebPlus must achieve the effect by creating and publishing a modified version of our image.

Other effects and operations that will cause recreation of an image include: cropping, rotation, most filter effects, recolouring, and significant overlaps of other objects.

5 Click ☒ **Close Preview** to return to the WebPlus workspace.

To recolour an image

1 Select the image and click the 🖼 **Re-colour Picture** button on the Picture context toolbar.

2 In the **Fill** dialog, click a black colour swatch and then click **OK**.

3 Try experimenting with other colours, for example, create a sepia tone effect by applying a brown or dark orange fill colour.

This creates an 'old photo' effect and can work well with the Photo Edge Effects used in the previous section.

To apply an image adjustment

- With the image selected, on the Picture context toolbar, click
  ☾ **Increase Contrast**. Repeat as required.

- (Optional) Experiment with the other adjustments provided on the
  Picture context toolbar to see how they affect your images.

🐾 Advanced image adjustments

PagePlus includes a powerful mix of
advanced image correction and
adjustment tools— including levels,
colour balance, channel mixer, HSL,
and Unsharp Mask—and a selection of
creative effects such as Diffuse Glow
and Gaussian Blur. All of these are
applied from the **PhotoLab** dialog,
which you can open by clicking

⦿ **PhotoLab** on the Picture context
toolbar.

For more information, see online Help.

Using frames

Placing empty picture frames on your site pages has several benefits:

- You can use them as 'placeholder' areas when you know you want to
  add images, but aren't quite sure of which ones to use.

- Frames make it easy to place images at a specific size or shape, without
  changing the aspect ratio—useful for 'contact' pictures or thumbnails.

- You can easily swap the images displayed inside frames without altering
  the page layout in any way.

To add a picture frame

1   On the Tools toolbar, on the 🖼 ▾ Picture flyout, click ⊠ **Empty
    Picture Frame**.

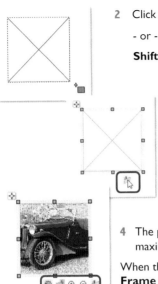

2   Click and drag to create a rectangular frame.

- or -

Shift-click and drag to create a square frame.

To add a single picture to a frame

1   Click to select the picture frame, then click the **Replace Picture** button in the lower-right corner of the frame.

2   In the **Import Picture** dialog, browse to your **Workspace** folder.

3   Select the **MG.jpg file** and click **Open**.

4   The picture is added to the frame and scaled to maximum-fit by default.

When the picture is selected, note that the **Picture Frame** toolbar displays in the lower-right corner. You can use these tools to adjust your picture inside the frame.

To adjust a picture inside a frame

- To reposition the picture inside the frame, click **Pan**, and then click and drag on the picture with the **Pan** cursor.

- To rotate the picture counter-clockwise, in 90° increments, click **Rotate**.

- To zoom in or out of the picture, click **Zoom In** or **Zoom Out**, and then click on the picture.

- To replace the picture, click **Replace Picture**, browse to and select a new picture and click **Open**.

- To change the scale options, on the Picture context toolbar, click **Frame Properties** and change the option in the dialog.

Image formats, ALT & TITLE text

Finally, we'll discuss another consideration when importing images and using drawn objects or 'fancy' text—**image formats**.

Imported images can have a variety of image formats (WebPlus supports the import of many different image formats), but most current Web browsers can only display **GIFs**, **JPGs**, and **PNGs**.

Images imported in one of these three Web-friendly formats may be published in their original format, untouched by WebPlus's intelligent image converter.

When necessary, WebPlus converts objects and images into a suitable format.

However, for drawn objects, modified artistic text, and imported images, you can set the individual or global image conversion options for your preferred published results.

Image compression formats

PNG is a 'lossless' format, which means that the quality does not suffer at the hands of built-in compression when the image is created.

JPEG/JPG files can be smaller than PNGs but JPEG compression can adversely affect quality.

GIF supports a single level of transparency (each pixel is either on or off) but the file format is restricted by only supporting 256 colours, which is fine for simple graphics but often unsuitable for photos.

For more information on the various file types, see online Help.

Let's see how you can modify both global and individual image export settings, starting with global settings.

To set global image export options

1   On the **File** menu, click **Site Properties**.

    In the **Site Properties** dialog, the **Graphics** tab offers global options for handling graphics when publishing your site.

For the ultimate in finding the right balance between file size and image quality for your site's images, consider exporting them from a program that offers a full **Export Optimizer** with export quality and file size preview, such as Serif PhotoPlus.

If you have PhotoPlus 10 or later installed, click the ⊕ **Edit in PhotoPlus** button on the Picture context toolbar to open the image for editing.

By default:

- Generated graphics (drawn objects, text with non-solid fills, objects with transparency or filter effects, or cropped/rotated objects) will be exported as PNG for best quality.

- JPGs will be exported as JPGs, even when resampled (you can adjust the compression for resampled JPGs).

2 Click **OK** to close the **Site Properties** dialog.

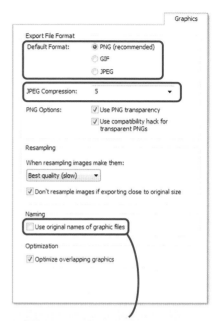

You can also override the default settings for particular images. This can be useful when you want a specific format to be output or to create ALT and TITLE text.

Note that when the original file is used, it will be renamed unless you select the **Use original names of graphic files** check box.

ALT and TITLE text is important to use to ensure that your website is accessible to everyone.

To set individual export options

1 Right-click on the large car picture and choose **Image Export Options...**

2 In the dialog, on the **Image Export Options** tab, you can override the global image publishing options by defining an image format for the selected object.

3 Click the **Alt and Title** tab. Here, you can enter pop-up TITLE and ALT text.

- TITLE text is the tooltip text that will appear when site visitors hover over the image in their Web browsers. This text is often used when clicking on a image has some function, for example, opening a larger version of the image in a new window.

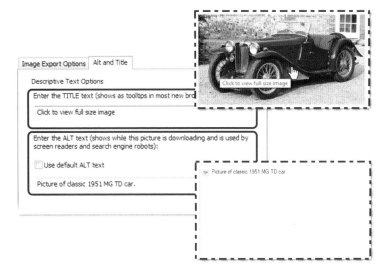

- ALT text, used to describe the content and/or purpose of an image, is the text that will appear in the area of your page where the image will download. (Note that ALT text should *not* be used for images whose only purpose is decorative.)

By default, the **Use default ALT text** option is selected. This tells WebPlus to use the TITLE text as the ALT description so that you only have to enter it once. By clearing the check box (as we have done) you can have different ALT and TITLE text. You can also choose to only have ALT text.

In order to accurately reproduce your design as a Web page, it is possible that items you create in WebPlus will be published as images. To allow for this, ALT and TITLE options are available for regular WebPlus objects as well as for imported images.

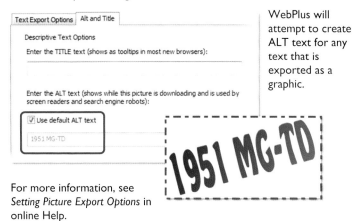

WebPlus will attempt to create ALT text for any text that is exported as a graphic.

For more information, see *Setting Picture Export Options* in online Help.

We suggest that you experiment with ALT and TITLE text and preview your results. ALT text is an important consideration when making your site accessible to as many people as possible, and it may even help improve your site's rankings in search engine results.

In this tutorial, we've explored some image import options, some efficiency and quality issues, and some publishing considerations.

Related tutorials and projects include: *Hyperlinks*, and *Web-Friendly Sites* (available from the Learning Zone in PDF format).

Colour Schemes

When designing your website, one of the most important factors to consider is colour.

But how do you select a colour palette that's right for your site? In this tutorial, we'll demystify the process and show you a few different ways to choose a colour scheme for your projects. You'll learn how to:

- Apply a preset colour scheme from the Colour Scheme Designer.
- Modify an existing colour scheme.
- Create your own colour scheme from scratch.

Colour Schemes

In the first section of this tutorial, we'll apply scheme colours to individual elements on a site. We'll then show you how you can edit and modify scheme colours. Finally, we'll create a custom colour scheme from scratch.

Applying scheme colours to objects

You can apply a colour scheme at any point during the design process. Each publication can have just one colour scheme at a time and can easily switch from one to another.

To apply a colour scheme

1   From the WebPlus Startup Wizard, select **Create > Use Design Template** and select a template of your choice. Click **Open**.

2   On the Page context toolbar, click **Colour Scheme Designer** (or click **Tools**, then **Colour Scheme Designer**).

    In the **Colour Scheme Designer** dialog, click the **Colour Schemes** tab.

    You'll see an assortment of named schemes, each consisting of a few basic colours.

The **Scheme Manager** pane contains a library of the available colour schemes. The highlighted scheme and its colours are loaded in the **Site Colour Scheme** pane.

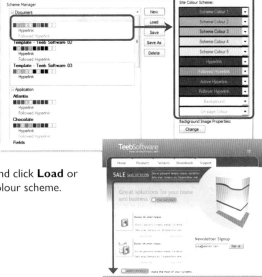

3   Select a different scheme and click **Load** or double-click the colour scheme.

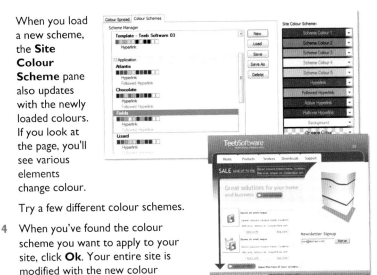

When you load a new scheme, the **Site Colour Scheme** pane also updates with the newly loaded colours. If you look at the page, you'll see various elements change colour.

Try a few different colour schemes.

4   When you've found the colour scheme you want to apply to your site, click **Ok**. Your entire site is modified with the new colour scheme.

So what exactly is happening here?

The scheme colours work like a paint-by-numbers system, where regions and elements of a page are coded with numbers. In each scheme, a specific colour is assigned to each number.

When you switch to a different scheme, any elements that have been assigned one of the scheme colour numbers are updated with the corresponding colour from the new scheme. Let's see this in action…

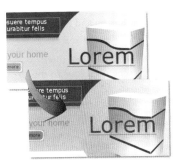

5   On the Tools toolbar, click the **A Artistic Text** tool and create a large text object on your page.

By default, new text objects are assigned to Scheme Colour 1.

6   Click **Tools**, then **Colour Scheme Designer** and switch to a different colour scheme.

Notice that the colour of your new text object changes.

Let's try the same experiment with a QuickShape.

7   On the Tools toolbar, click the 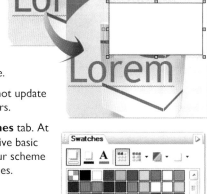 **Quick Rectangle** and draw a shape on your page.

    By default, the shape will have a white fill with a black outline.

8   Open the **Colour Scheme Designer** and switch to a different scheme.

    This time, the object does not update with the new scheme colours.

9   Click to display the **Swatches** tab. At the bottom of the tab, the five basic colours in the current colour scheme appear as numbered swatches.

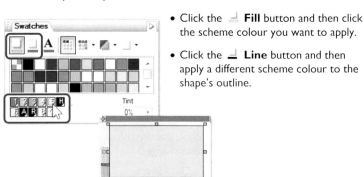

The colours for **Hyperlink**, **Followed Hyperlink**, **Active Hyperlink, Rollover Hyperlink, Background** and **On-page colour** display with the labels H, F, A, R, B and O.

10 Select your shape, then on the **Swatches** tab:

    • Click the ⊒ **Fill** button and then click the scheme colour you want to apply.

    • Click the ⊒ **Line** button and then apply a different scheme colour to the shape's outline.

Now let's see what happens when we switch colour schemes...

11 Click 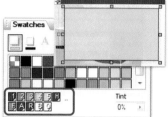 **Colour Scheme Designer**, and choose a different colour scheme.

In the WebPlus workspace, your shape is updated with the new scheme colour.

Notice too that the colour scheme swatches at the bottom of the **Swatches** tab have been replaced with the new colours.

As you can see, when you create new elements in a web template site, or start a site from scratch, you can extend a colour scheme to the new objects using the process just described.

If you copy an object that uses scheme colours to another site, the object will take on the new site's colour scheme.

You'll need to spend some time working out which colour combinations look best, but the mechanics of the process are simple.

Custom colour schemes

If you've tried various colour schemes but haven't found one that's quite right for your site, you can modify any of the colours in an existing scheme to create a new one.

To modify a pre-defined colour scheme

1 Click 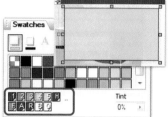 **Colour Scheme Designer** and then, click the **Colour Schemes** tab.

2 In the **Site Colour Scheme** pane, the current scheme colours are displayed.

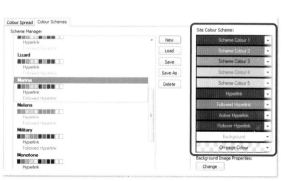

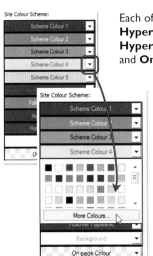

Each of the five scheme colour numbers (plus the **Hyperlink**, **Followed Hyperlink**, **Active Hyperlink**, **Rollover Hyperlink**, **Background** and **On-page Colour**) has its own drop-down list, showing available colours in the WebPlus palette.

3   To set or change a scheme colour, click to expand the drop-down list, and then select a new colour.

4   **Optional:** If the drop-down palette doesn't contain the colour you want to use, click **More Colours** to display the **Colour Selector**.

5   In the **Colour Selector** dialog, you can choose a colour to apply or mix your own custom colours.

• The **Models** tab displays the colour space of the currently selected colour model.

• The **Publication Palette** tab lets you modify the set of colours associated with the current site.

You can extend the Colour Selector's **Publication Palette** tab using the **Palette Manager**, which lets you modify the site's current palette and also load and save named palettes.

For more information, see *Managing Colours and Palettes* in online Help.

6   When you have modified your scheme, click **OK** to apply it to your document.

When you save your site, its current colour scheme is saved with the project file. However, if you want to use the scheme in other projects, you need to save it to the library.

To save a scheme to the Scheme Manager library

1   Click  **Colour Scheme Designer** and click the **Colour Schemes** tab.

2   In the **Site Colour Scheme** pane, the current document scheme colours are displayed.

3   To create a new scheme, click **Save As** and type in a new name.

- or -

To overwrite an existing scheme, click to select it and then, click **Save**.

4   The scheme library is updated to reflect the changes. If you have created a new scheme, it will appear at the bottom of the list in **Scheme Manager** pane.

In future, you will be able to load your saved scheme from within any project.

Each site stores a locally defined scheme, which may or may not correspond to a named scheme. The **Scheme Manager** pane displays a library of saved scheme colours that can be applied to any project file. When you modify a scheme in the library, it does not change any project files that were using the original scheme colours, they are preserved with the site. If you want to update the site to a modified scheme, you need to load it from the **Scheme Manager** pane and click **OK**.

Creating colour schemes from images

There may be times when you want to create a new colour scheme from scratch, perhaps using colours from your company logo or an image on your website.

To complete this section, you can use our sample photograph or any image of your choice. You'll find the sample photograph, **Cocktail.jpg**, in the **Workspace** folder of your WebPlus installation directory. In a standard installation, this folder is copied to the following location:

C:\Program Files\Serif\WebPlus\X4\Tutorials

To create a custom colour scheme from an image

1 On the **Tools** toolbar, click ▦ **Import Picture** and browse to locate the image you want to use.

Click **Open**, and then click and drag to place the image on your page.

2 Select the image and then on the Picture context toolbar, click
   ◉ **PhotoLab**.

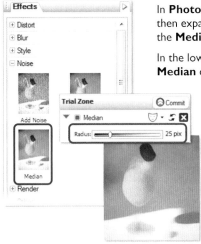

In **PhotoLab**, click the **Effects** tab and then expand the **Noise** category. Click the **Median** thumbnail.

In the lower right **Trial Zone**, the **Median** control displays,

3 Drag the **Radius** slider, to the right so that colours making up the image blend into colour 'blocks,' as illustrated.

Click ◉ **Commit** when you are happy with the result.

4 To close **PhotoLab** and return to the WebPlus workspace, click **OK**.

5 Back in the WebPlus workspace, on the Tools toolbar, select the ⬜ ▾ **Quick Rectangle** and draw a small square on your page (ours was about 60 x 60 pixels).

6 Select the shape, hold down the **Ctrl** key, and then drag to the right to create a copy.

7 Repeat the previous step to create five identical squares.

8 Select the first square, click the **Colour** tab, and then click the ✐ **Colour Picker**.

9 On the image, click and drag to select the first colour you want to add to your new colour scheme.

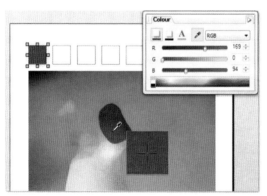

The popup colour sample updates as you drag to different areas of the image.

When you are happy with the colour displayed in the sample, release the mouse button.

The selected colour is applied to the square and added to the **Swatches** tab.

10 Selecting each of the remaining squares in turn, repeat the previous step to fill the shapes with four additional colours from your image.

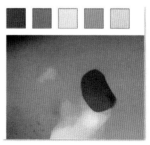

💡 You don't have to use QuickShapes to display your selected colours, but we think it's useful to see the colour swatches next to each other and the image on the page.

This allows you to determine if the colours work together with the image, and when isolated from the image. You can quickly and easily adjust the colours, pick new ones, or change the colour order, before deciding on your final scheme colours.

We used five squares—one for each main scheme colour—but you can create more than this to begin with. Once you've filled your squares with a selection of colours you can then decide on your final palette.

11 On the **Swatches** tab, scroll to the end of the palette swatches to find your new custom colours displayed.

We're now ready to create our new colour scheme.

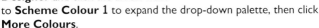

12 Open the **Colour Scheme Designer** and click the arrow next to **Scheme Colour 1** to expand the drop-down palette, then click **More Colours**.

In the **Colour Selector** dialog, click the **Publication Palette** tab and scroll to the end of the palette list to find your custom colours.

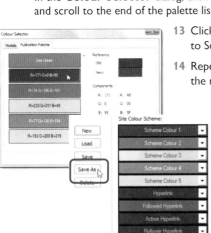

13 Click the colour you want to assign to Scheme Colour 1 and click **OK**.

14 Repeat the previous step to assign the remaining scheme colours.

15 Click **Save As** and type a name for your colour scheme.

16 Click **OK** to exit the dialog.

💡 When you save a colour scheme, it becomes available to all WebPlus publications.

The WebPlus colour schemes are designed with colours arranged from left to right, darkest to lightest, starting with Scheme Colour 1. The templates, theme objects, and samples are designed with this in mind so you'll notice that backgrounds are generally assigned the lightest of the scheme colours.

When creating your schemes, you'll get the best results if you follow this standard:

1 Start with the darkest colour and assign it to Scheme Colour 1.

2 Choose the next darkest colour for Scheme Colour 2.

Continue like this until you finish by assigning the lightest colour to Scheme Colour 5, or to the Background colour if you are using this.

To load a custom colour scheme

1 Click  **Colour Scheme Designer** and then, click the **Colour Schemes** tab.

2 On the **Colour Schemes** tab, select your new colour scheme and click **Load**. Click **OK**.

3 Click the **Swatches** tab. Note that the swatches at the bottom of the tab now display your custom scheme colours.

You can use these swatches to apply scheme colours to objects on your web pages.

Colour theory

If you have a basic colour in mind for your site, but you're not sure which colours to use with it, try the **Colour Spread** tab. Here you can create a complete colour scheme in minutes—choose your base colour, select a **Spread type**, and click **Populate**. WebPlus does the rest for you based on colour theory principles! For more information on how to use the **Colour Spread** pane, see online Help. To learn more about colour theory, see the *Designing With Colour* tutorial (available from the Learning Zone in PDF format).

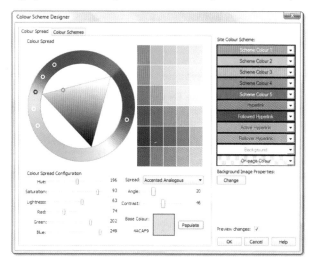

Congratulations, you've created a custom colour scheme from scratch! It's a relatively simple process, but one which we hope you'll find useful in your future website designs.

Navigation Bars

Having fantastic content on your website is useless unless your visitors can get to it! This makes a navigation bar an essential item. Luckily, WebPlus includes a wide range of professionally-designed and fully-customizable navigation bars for you to use.

In this exercise, you'll learn how to:

- Work with master page elements.
- Add, replace and customize navigation bars.
- Add multiple navigation bars and a sitemap.

If you're unfamiliar with website structure, we suggest you review the basic concepts before beginning this tutorial. See *Understanding site structure and navigation* in online Help or the *Site Structure* tutorial.

Navigation Bars

Navigation bars are essential to successful site navigation. Your visitors would be lost without them! You can create a simple navigation bar by creating a line of plain-text hyperlinks on every page, which link to the main pages of your website. However, these can look a little uninteresting and can be time consuming to set up, especially if you make changes to your website. Luckily for us, WebPlus has a whole host of professionally designed dynamic navigation bars for us to use, and the process is easy. We'll begin by replacing one of the navigation bars in a design template.

To replace a navigation bar on the page

1   From the **Startup Wizard**, click **Use Design Template**.

2   In the **Interest** category, click the **Reactive** template and click **Open**.

The template opens in the workspace. Notice the navigation bar at the top of the Home page.

Normally. The main navigation bar is shared by all of the pages on a website. As a result, the navigation bar is usually placed on the underlying master page. This means that you only have to place the navigation bar once, even though it appears on each page. Let's look at this now.

3   At the top of the **Site** tab, click the **Master Pages** button to display the master pages for the site, and then, double-click the **Master A** icon.

4   On the Master page, click to select the existing navigation bar and press the **Delete** key.

5   On the Web Objects toolbar, click **Insert Navigation Bar**.

6   In the **Navigation Bar Settings** dialog:

    • From the **Type** drop-down list, select **Designer (JavaScript)**, and then select the second design in the pane.

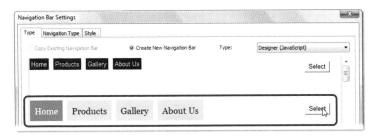

    • Click **OK** to accept the default settings.

7   Drag the new navigation bar into position next to the 'Search' box on the page.

8   Click  ▾ **Preview Site in {your browser of choice}**. Notice that the navigation bar has updated throughout the site, even though we only changed it once, This is because it is placed on the master page.

    If you click on the different page menu items, you'll notice that the navigation bar's appearance will vary depending on which page you're viewing.

To replace the navigation bar

1   On the **Site** tab, double-click the **Master A** icon to display the master page.

2 Right-click on the navigation bar object and click **Edit Navigation Bar...** (You can also double-click the navigation bar to edit it.)

3 In the dialog:

- Click the **Type** tab and select the **Create New Navigation Bar** option.

- Select a **Type** from the drop-down list (e.g., **Designer (Flash)**).

- Choose a navigation bar style and click **Select.**

The navigation bar is updated throughout the site with the new style.

4 Click 🖥 ▾ **Preview Site in {your browser of choice}** to see the effect.

Creating your own style

Now let's customize one of the pre-designed navigation bars to create the navigation bar used in the **Workspace scuba.wpp** site. First of all, we need to delete the existing navigation bar.

To prepare the Workspace file

1 On the Standard toolbar, click 📂 **Open**.

2 Navigate to the **Workspace** folder and click to select the **scuba.wpp** project file. In a typical installation, this folder is found in:

C:\Program Files\Serif\WebPlus\X4\Tutorials

3 Click **Yes** in the dialog to open as a new, untitled site.

4   Click **File > Save As...** and save your new file under a new name.

5   On the **Site** tab, double-click the **Master A** icon to display the master page.

6   Select the navigation bar and the object underneath it, and press the **Delete** key.

We're now ready to recreate the navigation bar.

To create the gel navigation bar

1   On the ☐ ▾ QuickShapes flyout, click the **Quick Rectangle** and then click and drag on the page to create a rectangle like the one below.

   • Drag the left node down to round the corners.

   • On the **Line** tab, in the line style drop-down list, select **None**.

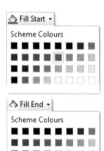

2   On the Tools toolbar, click the ◇ **Fill Tool**.

   • On the context toolbar, select **Linear** in the **Fill Type** drop-down list.

   • In the **Fill Start** drop-down list, select swatch 5 on the Scheme 2 row.

   • In the **Fill End** drop-down list, select swatch 8 on the Scheme 4 row.

   • Adjust the fill path by clicking and dragging the fill path end node to the top of the shape, and the fill path start node to the mid-point.

To add a navigation bar

1   On the Web Objects toolbar, click ▦ **Insert Navigation Bar**.

2   In the **Navigation Bar Settings** dialog::

   • On the **Type** tab, in the **Basic (Javascript)** category, select the third navigation bar in the list.

   • On the **Navigation Type** tab, **Top Level** is selected by default.

   • Click **OK**.

3   Drag the navigation bar into position on top of the gel object we created in the previous steps.

The navigation bar looks ok, but the default text colour is difficult to read against the gel button background. We'll change this now.

To customize the text style

1   Right-click the navigation bar object and click **Edit Navigation Bar...**

2   Click to display the **Style** tab. Notice that a dynamic preview of the navigation bar displays at the bottom of the dialog.

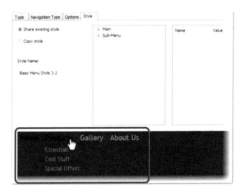

3   In the centre pane, click to expand the **Main** category. The rightmost pane contains the current settings for the currently selected (highlighted) element.

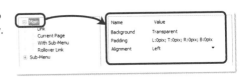

4   In the centre pane, click the **Link** sub-category, then, in the rightmost pane, double-click the **Text Style** value.

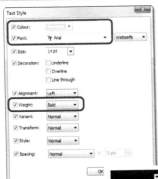

5   In the **Text Style** dialog:

    • Change the **Colour** to **Scheme Colour 5**.

    • Change the **Font** to **Arial**.

    • Change the **Weight** to **Bold**.

    • Click **OK**.

The navigation bar preview updates to match the changes.

Products   Gallery   About Us

6   In the centre pane, in the **Main** category, click the **Current Page** sub-category. In the rightmost pane, double click the **Text Style** value and in the **Text Style** dialog, change the colour to **Hyperlink (H)**. Click **OK**.

The navigation bar preview updates once again. The bar is looking much better, but we still need to adjust the **Rollover** colour and the menu items.

7 Repeat Step 6 to set the **Rollover Link** colour to **Rollover (R)**. The text will now turn orange when you hover over a menu item on the navigation bar preview.

The **Sub-Menu** on our navigation bar is still very low contrast in relation to our background. Luckily the procedure to adjust it is exactly the same.

8 In the centre pane, click to expand the **Sub-Menu** category. Apply the following settings:

- **Link**—Change the **Background** to the **Background** scheme colour swatch. Change the **Text Style** to **Scheme Colour 5**, **Arial** font and **Bold** weight.

- **Current Page**—Change the colour to **Scheme Colour 5**.

- **Rollover Link**—Change the colour to **Rollover (R)**

9 Verify your changes in the navigation bar preview. If you are happy with the result, click **OK**.

The navigation bar is updated on the master page.

10 Click ⌨ ▾ **Preview Site in {your browser of choice}** to see the effect.

The Flash™ and Javascript navigation bars have slightly different options to modify the style. In this tutorial, we've discussed modifying a Javascript navigation bar. Flash based navigation bars are also customized from the **Style** tab in the **Navigation Bar Settings** dialog. For more information on this and about other editing options, see *Adding navigation bars* in online Help.

Other types of navigation bar

In most websites, the main navigation bar is kept fairly simple, showing only the main, top-level pages of the website. This is to make it easier for you visitor to find the main pages. However, it is not uncommon to have several types of navigation bar used throughout your website. WebPlus makes this process very easy—it is even possible to maintain a consistent look throughout by sharing navigation bar styles between navigation bars. We don't have time to go into that now, but you can find out more about this and the **Navigation Manager**, in the *Navigation Manager* topic in online Help.

We'll conclude this tutorial by looking at a few examples from a completed version of our scuba website. However, we won't go into step-by-step detail—the general formatting process is much the same as the steps we followed to create our top-level navigation earlier in the tutorial.

Example I - Child Level navigation bar

On our website we have a **Top Level**, 'About Us' page which contains three child pages.

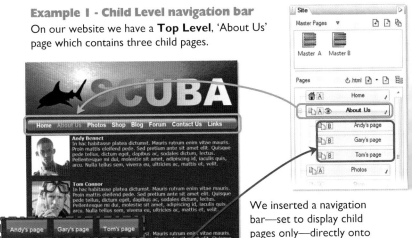

We inserted a navigation bar—set to display child pages only—directly onto the 'About Us' page.

To add a **Child Level** navigation bar, select the option on the **Navigation Type** tab in the **Navigation Bar Settings** dialog.

This bar has been formatted so that there is no 'current page' highlight, as it is only showing the pages beneath it in the site structure.

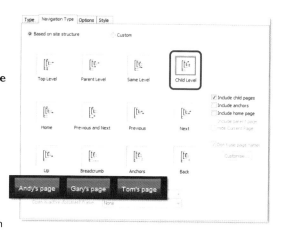

This form of navigation allows the visitor to get to relevant pages on the site, without delving through menus. It also makes it plainly obvious that there is more content to see.

Example 2 - Same Level navigation bar

Each of the diver's personal pages has a **Same Level** navigation bar. This makes it easy for the visitor to jump between these child pages, without having to use the drop-down list off the main navigation bar. It also makes it obvious at a glance that there is more to explore.

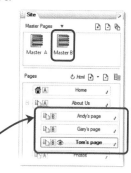

The bar itself has been added to a **Master B** page which is assigned only to the child pages.

To add a **Same Level** navigation bar, select the option on the **Navigation Type** tab in the **Navigation Bar Settings** dialog.

This is formatted to appear the same as the previous Child Level navigation bar on the 'About Us' page.

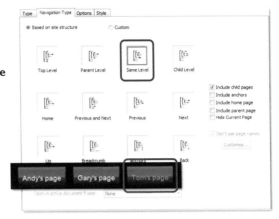

However, we have modified the original style to show the current page as an orange highlight, in-keeping with the other navigation elements.

Example 3 - Sitemap

Our final navigation example is a sitemap. This is a special type of navigation element that displays every page in your site. It allows visitors to jump straight to any page and can help to elevate your site's status within search engines.

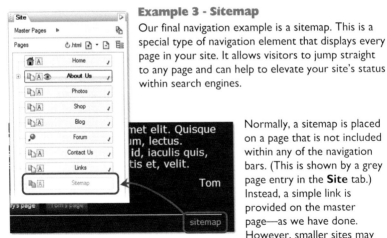

Normally, a sitemap is placed on a page that is not included within any of the navigation bars. (This is shown by a grey page entry in the **Site** tab.) Instead, a simple link is provided on the master page—as we have done. However, smaller sites may place a sitemap at the bottom of a master page.

Detailed information on using sitemaps in your site is included in the **How To** tab. See the topic in *Setting up navigation: Adding a navigation site map.*

To add a **Sitemap** navigation bar, in the **Navigation Bar Settings** dialog:

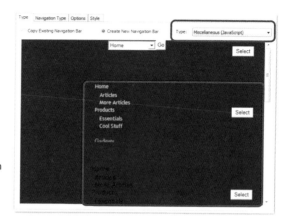

- In the **Type** drop-down list, choose **Miscellaneous (Javascript)**. Choose from either navigation bar two or three in the list.

- On the **Navigation Type** tab, ensure that the **Include anchors** check box is selected if you have used anchors in your site.

- Set the options and style and then click **OK**.

The sitemap is placed on the page.

Well, that concludes this tutorial. We hope this exercise has convinced you of the versatility of navigation bars that not only adapt to your site structure but blend harmoniously with your site's visual design.

Equipped with a basic knowledge of these remarkable WebPlus features, you're ready to create your own website layouts. Now it's up to you and your imagination!

Previewing & Publishing

Having gone to some trouble to make a site—even simple sites take a certain amount of time and effort—it's time to publish to the Internet.

In this tutorial we will show you how to:

- Use the Preview toolbar to preview your site.

- Preview your site at different resolutions and in different Web browsers.

- Publish and maintain your website.

Previewing & Publishing

Whether you have a simple text-based website or a beautifully crafted work of art, you want to know that people will see your site in the way that you intended. Before you upload your site to the masses, the first step is to preview your work in a web browser.

To preview your site in WebPlus

1   From the WebPlus Startup Wizard, choose **Create > Use Design Template**, and open the template of your choice.

2   Click the arrow to expand the ⊟ ▾ **Preview Site** drop-down list. Click the first option, **Preview in Window**.

    (If you have created a large site, there may be a slight delay while the site is exported to display in a web browser.)

    Once exported, WebPlus displays the site preview in a built-in Microsoft Internet Explorer window.

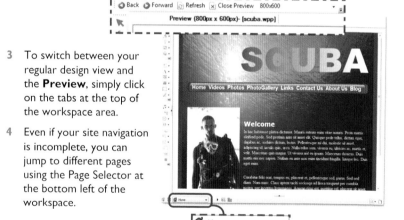

3   To switch between your regular design view and the **Preview**, simply click on the tabs at the top of the workspace area.

4   Even if your site navigation is incomplete, you can jump to different pages using the Page Selector at the bottom left of the workspace.

💡 Checking your site with different screen resolutions is easy in the **Preview** window. Simply pick another preview size in the drop-down list on the context toolbar. This allows you to determine how much of your page width is visible at certain resolutions, and can help you to decide on page width and length, and position of navigation elements.

5   When you have finished, click **Close Preview**.

If you make any changes to your design, your site will be 'republished' when you next switch to the **Preview**. You can also preview your site, or a page within your site, in an actual browser window. This is useful for testing compatibility with other browsers such as Mozilla Firefox, Safari or Opera. WebPlus automatically detects if alternate browsers are installed.

To preview your site in a Web browser

1   Click the arrow to expand the 🖵 ▾ **Preview Site** drop-down list.

2   Select **Preview Site in {your web browser of choice}**.

3   Your site will open in a new browser window.

If you have installed a browser that does not appear in the Preview List, you may need to add it manually. For more information see *Previewing your website* in online Help.

It's worth being aware that Internet Explorer (6, 7 and 8 combined) and Mozilla Firefox are the most popular Web browsers, but they can behave very differently. Other browsers such as Opera (especially for mobile devices) and Safari are also supported by WebPlus.

Mozilla Firefox

Internet Explorer

Safari

Opera

We'll assume that our design looks great in a range of browsers. Now it's time to publish our site and make our presence known on the Internet. Even though you may have saved your website as a WebPlus project, it's not truly a 'website' until you've converted it to files that can be viewed in a Web browser. WebPlus does this automatically when you publish the site.

Note: The next steps assume that you have dedicated space on a web server. If you are unsure how to access this, contact your service provider.

To publish to the Web

1   Check your page names, file names, and picture export settings in the **File > Site Properties...** and **Format > Image Export Options...** dialogs.

    (For details, see *Setting page and file names* and *Setting picture export options* in online Help.)

2   Use **Site Checker** to check your site for problems such as non-websafe fonts, invalid anchors and hyperlinks, and so on. (See *Using Site Checker* in online Help.)

3   On the Standard toolbar, click 🔟 **Publish to Web**.

4   The first time you publish to the web, the **WebPlus.net Web Hosting** dialog will be displayed:

    • Click **Setup Hosting** to sign up for a Serif web hosting account..

    • Login to **Serif Web Resources**. If you haven't yet created an account, click **Create Account**. (See the *Counters & Polls* tutorial, and online Help.)

    • Activate your hosting. For more information, see *Using Serif web hosting* in online Help.

5   Click **Create Hosting**. The dialog confirms that your account has been created and your account details have been saved into WebPlus.

    Exit the **Create a Serif Web Resources and Hosting Account** dialog.

    -or-

    Click **Manage Hosting** to check your account information, then click **Exit**.

    The **Publish to Web** dialog displays your FTP account details.

6   In the **Page Range** tree, select which page(s) to publish. To publish the entire site, select the **Publish All Pages** option. Click **OK**.

Setting up manual FTP

1 To set up a manual FTP account for the first time, using account details given by your own Internet Service Provider, click **No Thanks** in the **WebPlus.net Web Hosting** dialog.

2 In the **Publish to Web** dialog, click **Accounts...**, then click **Add...** to open the **Account Details** dialog.

   When publishing to the Web (or uploading it manually using FTP software) you'll need to provide the following information, most of which you can obtain from your Internet Service Provider (ISP) or Web host:

- **Account name:** A descriptive name for this connection. This can be any name of your choice. You'll use it to identify this account in WebPlus (you may have more than one).

- **FTP address:** The URL (path), similar to a Web address, that locates the Internet-based server that will store your files.

- This will start with 'ftp://' and is supplied by your service provider.

- **Port number:** Unless directed by your provider, leave the **Port number** set at 21. This is the default port used by most FTP servers for file transfer.

- **Folder:** Allows you to upload sites to sub-folders of your main website's address. You can leave this blank unless you are directed otherwise by your provider, or you want to publish to a specific subfolder of your root directory. (This may also be needed to correctly route your upload specifically to your own Web space.)

- **Username:** Specified by your ISP or Web host (and is often **case-sensitive**).

- **Password:** As for Username, this is normally the same information required for ISP or Web host account log-on, and is often case-sensitive.

- **Passive Mode:** Leave checked (by default) unless you experience upload problems.

- **Website URL:** The URL of your website—this is the 'address' where your site resides on the Web.

   For more information about setting up your account details, see *Publishing to the web* in online Help

3 When you've entered all your information, click **OK**.

4 Click **Update Account**, your new FTP account and settings are displayed in the **Publish to Web** dialog.

5 In the **Page Range** tree, select which page(s) to publish. To publish the entire site, select the **Publish All Pages** option. Click **OK**.

Publishing options

WebPlus can publish your site in several ways:

- **Publish to a Disk Folder -** lets you use your site as a network-based Intranet, write it to CD-ROM for distribution, or upload it manually to an Internet server using file transfer protocol (FTP) software.

- **Publish to the Web -** publish your page or site directly to a Web server so that it can be viewed over the Internet.

- **Quick Publish to Web** - publish only the page that you are currently working on directly to the Web server.

For more information, see online Help.

WebPlus will convert your design into HTML pages with associated graphics and other files, then begin to upload your site to the Internet, showing individual file progress and overall progress.

Subsequent uploads of your site to that account will allow you to perform either an **Incremental Update** or a **Full Upload**.

- **Incremental Update:** If you choose this option, WebPlus will export your site and compare the exported files to those already on the server. It will only upload files that are new or have changed since the last upload. This option can also check for missing files. Incremental updates are great when you want to quickly replace minor elements of your site!

- **Full Upload:** If you choose this option, WebPlus will upload all the files, regardless of whether they have changed since the last upload.

In both cases you can instruct WebPlus to delete uploaded files that are no longer required by selecting this option in the dialog.

If your web server cannot accommodate spaces in file names, complete the following steps to have WebPlus remove the spaces and symbols from file names when they are published:

1 On the **File** menu, click **Site Properties**.

2 Click the **Options** tab and then select the **Remove spaces** and **Remove symbol character** options.

3 If you've already published your site, you'll need to republish to fix the problem. This also improves site reliability.

Web pages are normally published with lower case file names. In the same dialog select **Make lower case** to get WebPlus to do this for you.

7 WebPlus exports the selected pages.

Close the **Uploading files** dialog—the **Website Publishing** dialog opens. To view your site online, choose your browser from the drop-down list and click **View this URL**.

That's it! You've published your site to the Web for all to see! As you can see, WebPlus makes it very easy to publish your site and upload new content.

Typically, the big subscription networks allocate to each user several megabytes of server space for a 'personal website,' and many plans are available from smaller ISPs. Once you've set up your account and can connect your computer to the host, publishing to the Web is simply a matter of transferring files.

The basic process of uploading files to a server is quite simple, as outlined above. However, some ISPs and Web hosts are better than others at providing the basic information you'll need the first time you publish to their server (ftp address, steps needed to connect to the server, any special requirements, and so on).

If you're having problems we suggest you check your provider's website to find the information you need, or contact their customer support team.

Note: Serif cannot supply you with this information unless you have a Serif web hosting account.

Dynamic Content

Aimed at both beginners and more experienced WebPlus users, these tutorials show you how to add dynamic content to your site.

Topics covered include Flash™ photo galleries and banners, as well as a selection of the smart objects hosted by Serif Web Resources.

Flash™ Photo Gallery

With WebPlus, you can add Flash™ photo galleries to your websites. Simply add your photos, and then choose from a range of professionally-designed templates. You can customize the templates to suit the theme of your photos, and even add background music!

In this tutorial, we'll show you how to:

- Add photos to a photo gallery.
- Add captions.
- Adjust photo brightness and contrast.
- Apply gallery styles and settings.
- Edit an existing photo gallery.

Flash Photo Gallery

In this exercise, we'll create a photo gallery using photographs taken on a visit to the zoo. If you want to use the same images, you'll find them in your **Workspace\Zoo** folder. In a standard installation, this folder is installed to the following location:

C:\Program Files\Serif\WebPlus\X4\Tutorials

We'll create our gallery on a new blank website, but you may want to add yours to an existing WebPlus project.

1   From the Startup Wizard, click **Create New > Blank Site**, or on the Standard toolbar, click ☐ **New Site**.

2   On the Standard Objects toolbar, on the 🖾 ▾ Picture flyout, click 🖾 **Insert Photo Gallery**.

3   In the **Photo Gallery** dialog, select the type of gallery you want to use.

- **Professional Flash Photo Gallery**
- **Flash Photo Gallery**
- **JavaScript Gallery**

🔍 **Professional Flash**, **Flash** and **JavaScript** photo galleries each offer different gallery styles and settings for you to determine user navigation.

Professional Flash is more suitable for displaying large photo collections—you can present your photos in multiple albums. It offers horizontal thumbnail rollover styles which enable you to define basic preferences, as well as settings for captions, navigation bars, albums and hyperlinks. By enabling advanced options you can also define your preferences for gallery transitions, timers, and text. You can load images into the gallery from an RSS 2.0 Media feed or SlideShowPro Director content system, and export your preferred gallery settings to file so that you can import them to use whenever you create a Professional Flash gallery.

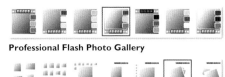

Professional Flash Photo Gallery

Flash Photo Gallery

Flash is ideal for displaying smaller photo collections and **JavaScript** is a suitable alternative to using flash on your site. They both offer horizontal and vertical thumbnail rollover, photo grid and photo stack styles. You can define settings for gallery position, thumbnails, navigation bars, captions and transitions. With Flash only, you can also add background music.

JavaScript Photo Gallery

The procedure for adding a photo gallery to your site is the same for all three types of gallery. For this exercise, we've selected a **Professional Flash Photo Gallery**.

4   Click **Next**. In the **Photo Gallery** dialog, click **Add Folder**.

5   In the **Browse For Folder** dialog, select the folder containing your photos and click **OK**.

Your photos display as thumbnails in the dialog.

> The **Flash Photo Galler**y dialog offers the following options for adding photos:
>
> • **Add Files:** Choose this option to add individual photos to your gallery.
>
> • **Add Folder:** Choose this option to add photos contained inside a folder on your computer.
>
> • **Add Twain:** Choose this option to add photos from a TWAIN source, such as a scanner or digital camera. (For details, see online Help.)

6   You can use the buttons running down the left side of the dialog to add more photos or delete photos that you no longer want.

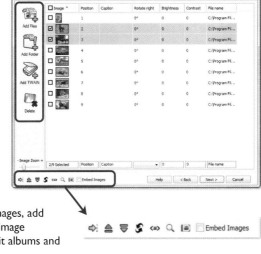

7   Use the buttons across the lower edge of the dialog to adjust image order, rotate images, add captions, make image adjustments, edit albums and embed images.

We want our photo gallery to begin with the photo of the giraffe's head. Currently this photo is last in the sequence so we need to move it.

8 Select the photo and then click **Move to Position**. In the **Move To** dialog, input the number 1 to move the photo to first place in the sequence. If you need to, zoom into your images using the **Image Zoom** slider.

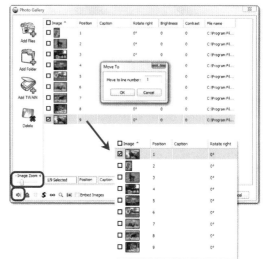

Now let's add some captions to our photos.

9 With the first photo still selected, click the **Caption** column.

10 In the **Caption** box type a caption for the selected photo.

-or-

To add the same caption to multiple photos, select their check boxes and type the caption into the box at the bottom of the **Caption** column.

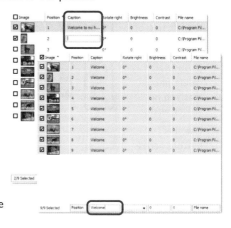

11 Repeat steps 9 and 10 to add captions to the remaining photos.

12 **Optional:** To adjust **Brightness** and **Contrast**, click in their respective columns and type values between -100 and 100.

-or-

To apply the same adjustment to multiple photos, select their check boxes and type a value into the boxes at the bottom of the **Brightness** and **Contrast** columns.

13 **Optional:** To embed your photos in the .wpp project file, select the **Embed Images** check box. (If you do not select this option your photos will remain 'linked' to the file.)

14 When you are happy with your photos and captions, click **Next**.

15 Click through the templates displayed in the **Gallery Style** pane.

As you do so:

- The **Preview** pane shows how your photos will appear with the selected gallery style applied.

- The settings pane updates to display the various options you can adjust for the selected gallery style.

16 Select the gallery style you prefer and then adjust the settings as required.

17 When you are happy with your photo gallery style and settings, click **Finish**.

- or -

To add or remove photos, click **Back** to return to the previous dialog. Make your changes, click **Next**, and then click **Finish**.

Click once on your page to insert the gallery at default size.

18 Optional:

- To resize the photo gallery, select it with the ➤ **Pointer Tool** and drag from a corner or line end handle. To constrain the photo gallery when resizing, hold down the **Shift** key when dragging.

- To move the position of the photo gallery on your page, select it with the ➤ **Pointer Tool** and drag.

19 To preview your photo gallery:

On the Standard toolbar, click 🖥 ▾ **Preview Site** and select **Preview Page in <your browser of choice>**.

Once you've inserted your photo gallery, it's easy to add and delete photos, switch to a different gallery style, and adjust settings.

To edit a photo gallery

1 Right click the photo gallery and click **Edit Photo Gallery**. -or-
Double-click the photo gallery using the ➤ **Pointer Tool**.

2 The **Photo Gallery** dialog opens.

3 Follow the steps outlined previously to fine-tune your gallery.

We've reached the end of this tutorial. In a few simple steps, we've created a stylish, professional-looking photo gallery. We're sure you'll enjoy experimenting with this powerful new feature—a great way to display treasured memories, or showcase those artistic shots you're particularly proud of!

Flash Objects

The WebPlus **Gallery** tab provides a wide range of predesigned Flash™ banners that you can add to your site, and customize to suit your needs.

In addition, it's very easy to add your own custom Flash objects to your WebPlus site.

In this tutorial we'll show you how to:

- Insert a custom Flash object into a WebPlus document.
- Fine-tune your Flash object.
- Add a predesigned WebPlus Flash banner to your site.

Flash Objects

Flash (*.swf) files are viewable movies using the Flash Player format. In WebPlus, you can see the effects of these files as soon as they are placed on your page, even without previewing.

To insert a custom Flash file

1   Open an existing WebPlus site, or create a new blank site.

2   On the **Insert** menu, choose **Media**, and then click **Flash**.

    - or -

    On the Web Objects toolbar, on the **Media** flyout, click ▣ **Flash...**

3   In the **Flash** dialog, click **Browse**, and then locate and select the .swf file you want to insert.

    You will find an example, **DaftDog.swf**, in your **Workspace** folder. In a standard installation, you'll find this in the following location:

    C:\Program Files\Serif\WebPlus\X4\Tutorials

    To keep the .swf file separate from the WebPlus file (using a link to the source file) clear the **Embed Flash file in site** option.

Optional step: You can also fine-tune your Flash object in this dialog.

For example, you can choose to:

*   Start the animation as soon as the page is loaded.

*   Loop the animation.

*   Set background transparency.

*   Add parameters—advanced functionality allowing modification of the object's behaviour on the completed page.

4   When you have selected the required options, click **OK**.

5   On the WebPlus page, you'll see the ⊕▦ **Picture Import** cursor.

Click to insert the file at its default size, or drag to set a custom size. You should see a preview of the file as you drag.

Remember, you can always resize a Flash object once you have placed it on your page.

Note that the valid parameters for Flash objects vary depending on the object itself. For details, see the documentation relating to your particular Flash object.

Congratulations! You have successfully added the Flash object to your website. Feel free to preview it in your favourite browser. Should you choose to publish your site to the Internet, WebPlus will automatically upload your Flash object for you; no additional work is required on your behalf.

Flash Banners

Web banners can be useful advertising tools. The following section shows you how to add and customize a predesigned WebPlus Flash banner on your site's master page.

To insert a predesigned Flash banner

1 Open the master page of your site and click the **Gallery** tab.

2 At the top of the tab, expand the drop-down menu, and then select the **Template Flash Banners** category.

3 Scroll to the **1 Image Slide In With Flicker** subcategory. You will see thumbnails of the various banner styles available.

4 Click on the **Photographer** thumbnail and drag it onto your master page.

5 Select the banner then on the **Align** tab, click ☞ **Centre Horizontally**.

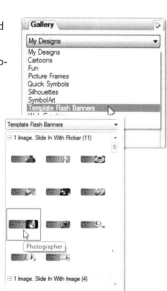

Currently, the title of the banner displays the company title that is set in the WebPlus **User Details** dialog.

Unless you have already edited the user details, the title displayed by default will be '**Your Company Name**'.

You can change this text by either updating the user details, or by editing the Flash banner. We'll show both methods.

To update the banner title by setting user details

1   Click outside of the page area to deselect everything, then on the Page context toolbar, click 🔳 **Set User Details**.

2   In the **User Details** dialog, change the company name to any name of your choice and click **Update**.

The banner updates with your new company name.

The **User Details** dialog is great for updating some text elements on your banner, such as your company name, address, or telephone number. But suppose you want to change the image—for example, to display a new product—or edit the bullet points to reflect recent new features or special offers.

💡 Store frequently-used or frequently-updated information in the **User Details** dialog. It will make updating data like mobile phone numbers or email addresses much easier! To insert a **user details** item:

1   Create a text frame on your page.

2   On the **Insert** menu, choose **Information**, then click **User Details**.

3   In the **User Details** dialog, select the line of text you want to insert and then click **OK**.

To edit Flash banner elements

1   Double-click the banner, or right-click and select **Edit Flash**.

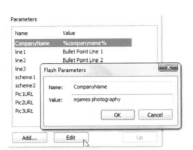

2   In the **Flash** dialog, in the **Parameters** pane, click to select the **CompanyName** element and then click the **Edit** button.

3   In the **Flash Parameters** dialog, in the **Value** box, delete the text (including the %) and type your company name. Click **OK**.

4   Repeat steps 2 and 3 to edit the bullet point text (line1, line2, and line3) as required.

5   When you've finished updating your text elements, click **OK** to close the **Flash** dialog and review your changes.

There may be times when you want to change other elements of your banner, such as the image, or even the colours.

You can use the same dialog to do this, as we'll now demonstrate.

6   Double-click the banner to open the **Flash** dialog.

7   In the right of the dialog, the **Additional Files** box lists the images used in the banner. (This particular banner only uses one image; others may use more.)

Click the **Add...** button and then browse to the mjames sample photo images provided in your ...**Workspace** folder.

In a standard installation, this folder is installed to the following location:

C:\\Program Files\\Serif\\WebPlus\\X4\\Tutorials

As this banner only uses one image, the image at the top of the list is the one that is displayed. We suggest you delete any unused files from the **Additional Files** list. While any 'extra' images will not display, they will still be included when you publish your site and will therefore take up Web server space unnecessarily.

For banners using two or three images, the images are displayed in the order they are listed in the **Additional Files** box.

8   Select the **clouds.png** file and click **Open**.

    The new file is added to the **Additional Files** list.

9   Select the **clouds.jpg** file in the list and click the **Up** button to move it to the top of the list.

10 Click **OK** to see your new image displayed in the banner.

Two and three image banners

The steps for inserting two and three image banners are very similar to adding a one image banner, there are just a couple of additional images!

1   Open a new site by choosing **File > New**.

2   From the **Gallery** tab, navigate to the **Template Flash Banners** category, and then the **2 Image Slide in with Flicker Image Swap** subcategory.

3   Click on the **Photographer** thumbnail and drag it onto your master page.

    You will notice that the banner has retained the User Details that you edited in the previous section.

4   Double-click the banner to open the **Flash** dialog.

5 In the **Additional Files** section on the right you'll see two .jpg files listed.

These are the image files that are currently displayed in the banner.

Click the **Add...** button and then in the **Open** dialog, browse to your **Tutorials\Workspace** folder. Select the **poppy head.jpg** file and click **Open**.

6 The new file is now listed in the **Additional Files** list box. Select it and click **Up** twice to move it to the top of the list.

7 Repeat steps **5-6** to add **droplet.jpg**.

8 To get the Flash banner to loop, ensure that the **Loop** option is checked.

9 Click **OK** and review your changes on the page.

Editing the banner colour scheme

1 Double-click the banner to reopen the **Flash** dialog.

2 In the parameters list, you'll see two elements labelled **scheme1** and **scheme2**. These elements link to colour swatches in the site's currently selected colour scheme.

We'll return to WebPlus colour schemes in more detail later. For the following steps, all you need to know is that the currently selected scheme colours for this site are displayed as numbered swatches at the bottom of the **Swatches** tab.

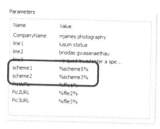

3   In the **Parameters** pane, select the **scheme1** element and click **Edit**.

4   In the **Flash Parameters** dialog, change the value to **%scheme5%**. Click **OK**.

5   Repeat the steps to change **scheme 2** to **%scheme3%**.

6   Click **OK** to close the **Flash** dialog and view your results.

You'll see that the text elements have been updated with your changes. In addition, the company name is now sitting on a green background, which corresponds to the **Scheme Colour 5** swatch on the **Swatches** tab.

By choosing scheme colours in this way, the Flash banner will also update whenever you change the colour scheme of the site.

These are just some of the things you can do with the banners. Feel free to experiment on your own!

Counters & Polls

In this tutorial, we'll introduce you to **Serif Web Resources** and the **Smart Objects** that you can use to easily add interactivity to your website.

In this tutorial, you'll learn how to:

- Sign up for **Serif Web Resources**.
- Insert and configure a hit counter.
- Insert and configure a poll.

Counters & Polls

It can be really useful to know how many visitors that your site is receiving. This is the main use of a hit counter.

A poll is another useful tool to collect information from your site visitors. Adding these object is easy when you use **Smart Objects**.

Over the next few pages, we'll show you how to sign up to an account and how to add, and manage a hit counter and a poll.

WebPlus provides a range of interactive and dynamic objects, which all 'collect' information from the object. These objects are known as **Smart objects** and are available from **Serif Web Resources**, a secure online service which not only 'hosts' the objects, but also stores the associated data on secure server space designated to Serif.

Setting up a Serif Web Resources account

To access the Smart objects, you need to log in to Serif Web Resources. If you don't have a valid username and password you must first create a Serif Web Resources account.

To create a Serif Web Resources account

1   On the Web Objects toolbar, click the 🍀 **Smart Object Tool**.

2   In the login dialog, click **Create Account**.

3   In the next dialog:

- Type your email address.

- Type your password twice.

- Type your screen name.

- Click **Signup**.

Note. If your email address is not already associated with a Serif account, you will be asked to provide a few extra details. Follow the instructions in the dialog.

4   A confirmation email is sent to your email address.

Click the link in the email and you're ready to access Serif Web Resources!

To access Serif Web Resources

1   On the Web Objects toolbar, click the the 🐾 **Smart Object Tool**.

2   In the login dialog:

- Type your username (email address).

- Type your password.

- **Optional:** Select **Remember account details**.

- Click the **Login** button.

The **Smart Objects** dialog opens.

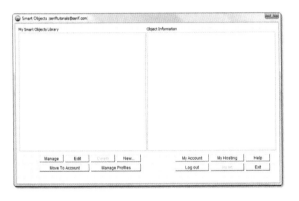

Note that Smart objects are not added directly to the page from Serif Web Resources, but are first added to an object library displayed in the left **My Smart Objects** pane. Currently, because we have yet to create any Smart objects, the library is empty.

The Smart objects library lets you manage and edit your objects and add them to your web pages immediately or later.

We're now ready to create our Smart objects.

Hit Counters

A **hit counter** provides an easy way to see how many visitors your site is attracting.

We added our hit counter to the **Home** page of our **Scuba.wpp** site. You can either work through this example using one of the **Workspace** project files or your own web page.

In a standard installation, the **Workspace** folder is installed to the following location:

C:\Program Files\Serif\WebPlus\X4\Tutorials

To add a hit counter to the library

1   In the **Smart Objects** dialog, beneath the **My Smart Objects Library** pane, click **New...**

2   In the **Create Smart Object** dialog, select the **Hit Counter** option and click **OK**.

3   In the dialog:

- Select a hit counter style.

- Type a name for your hit counter.

- Choose the number of digits to display.

- To ensure that multiple visits made by the same visitor in one day are only counted as a single hit, select **Filter Daily Duplicates**.

- In the **Email Frequency** box, specify how often you want to be notified of the count. For example, by default you will receive email notification each time the counter increments by a multiple of 1000.

- Click **Create** to add the hit counter object to the library.

In the **My Smart Objects** dialog, your hit counter is listed in the **My Smart Objects Library** pane.

To add a hit counter to the page

1 In the Library pane, select the hit counter and click **Insert**.

2 Position the cursor where you want the hit counter to appear and then click on the page. The hit counter previews automatically.

Great, we've added our first Smart object. We can use the same procedure to add the other Smart objects to our site. Before we go on, let's show you how to edit your hit counter.

You can edit Smart objects from the Smart Object Library or by right-clicking the object on the page.

To edit a hit counter

1 On the Web Objects toolbar, click the ⚙ **Smart Object** tool. (If necessary, log into your account.)

2 In the **Smart Objects** library, select the hit counter and click **Edit**.

3 Edit the hit counter as required.

4 Click **Save**.

To manage a hit counter

1 On the Web Objects toolbar, click the ⚙ **Smart Object** tool. (If necessary, log into your account.)

2 In the **Smart Objects** library, select the hit counter and click **Manage**.

The current count is displayed along with the date and time since counting began.

3 Click **Reset** to zero the counter.

4 Click **Save**.

💡 If your Smart objects do not preview on the page, you can turn previews on.

To turn Smart object previews on:

1 Click **Tools**, then **Options**.

2 In the **Options** dialog, expand the **Layout** category. In the **Layout** sub-category, select the **Preview Hosted Objects** check box and click **OK**.

Polls

A poll provides a great way for visitors to interact with your website and express their opinions. You can add as many poll objects to your website as you want, but they are best used sparingly so as not to put people off your site. The trick is to ask only the questions you really want the answers to!

We added our poll to a 'Survey' page that we created on our fictional SCUBA diving club site. A version of this project file, **scuba.wpp**, can be found in the **Workspace** folder. Alternatively, why not add a poll to your own web page?

To add a poll

1   Click the 🏵 **Smart Objects Tool**.

2   In the **Smart Objects** dialog, click **New...**

3   In the next dialog, select **Poll**, choose a **Language** option from the drop-down list, and then click **OK**.

4   In the **Create Smart Object** dialog:

- Name your object, e.g., SCUBA Poll.

- In the text box at the top of the dialog, type your poll question.

- In the boxes below, type the voting options you want to display.

- Use the other controls to adjust the appearance of the poll. You can change text colour, font, and size.

- Ensure the option to filter daily duplicates is checked.

- Click **Create** to add the poll object to your library.

5 Click **Insert** to add the poll to your page.

6 Position the ⊕▥ cursor where you want the poll to appear and then click on the page.

In our example, we added interest by using a QuickShape as a background for our Poll object.

7 Preview the page in your browser to see how your poll will appear to site visitors.

Each time a site visitor clicks on one of the options, the result is recorded by the smart object.

To view the results of your poll

1 On the Web Objects toolbar, click the ✿ **Smart Object Tool**. (If necessary, log into your account.)

2 In the **Smart Objects** library, select the poll and click **Manage**.

The results are displayed for each answer.

3 Click the link to reset a single poll option to 0.

- or -

Click **Reset All** to reset the votes to 0 for all poll options (or click **Exit** to leave without making any changes).

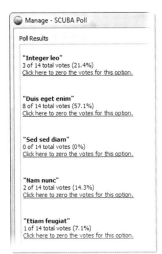

To edit your poll

1   On the Web Objects toolbar, click the 🐝 **Smart Object Tool**. (If necessary, log into your account.)

2   In the **Smart Objects** library, select the Poll and click **Edit**.

3   Edit as required.

4   Click **Save**.

You can have as many poll objects on your page as you want, so why not have a go at creating a questionnaire? Don't forget to have a look at the other tutorials in this section for a guide on using other smart objects such as forums and blogs.

Forms

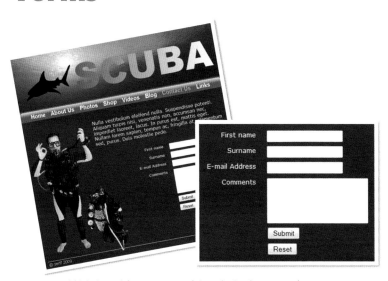

Web-based forms are useful tools. In this tutorial, we are going to create a simple form that allows site visitors to contact the webmaster and submit their personal comments.

You'll learn how to:

- Create a web-based email form using the **Form Wizard**.
- Edit form objects.

This tutorial assumes that you have already registered for a **Serif Web Resources** account. If you are unsure how to do this, see the tutorial *Counters & Polls* or online Help.

Forms

Forms are used to collect data from site visitors. Data collected can be as simple as the person's name and email address, or a whole host of personal information. How much data you ask for on a form really depends on what you need it for.

In this tutorial, we're going to add a contact form to a 'Contact Us' page that we created on our fictional SCUBA diving club site. A similar version of this project file, **scuba.wpp**, can be found in the **Workspace** folder.

In a standard installation, this folder is installed to the following location:

C:\Program Files\Serif\WebPlus\X4\Tutorials

Alternatively, why not add a form to your own web page?

Let's get started.

To create a form using the Form Wizard

1   Open the **Contact Us** page in the workspace by double-clicking it on the **Site** tab.

2   On the Web Objects toolbar, on the Forms flyout, click 🖼 **Form Wizard**.

3   In the first **Form Wizard** dialog, click **Use and adapt a standard form** and then click **Next**.

4   Click any list item to display a preview of the selected form in the **Preview** pane.

Select the **Comments 2** form and click **Next**.

5   The next dialog allows you to customize the form layout. Here, you can edit and delete the existing form controls, or add new ones (see the note on the next page).

The default form suits our purpose so click **Next** to proceed.

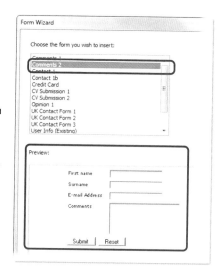

The building blocks of a form comprise a mixture of text, graphics, and **form controls**. Form controls collect visitor data and can be added, moved, and modified in a similar way to other WebPlus objects.

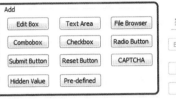

Form control fields include buttons, text boxes, check boxes, radio buttons, combo boxes, and so on. A typical form is made up of a combination of these fields.

The **Form options** also include a CAPTCHA object. When linked to your Serif Web Resources account, this anti-spamming control can help to prevent junk email from non-human web traffic. The site visitor must type the graphical word into the input field. If they match, the visitor is allowed to continue.

Randomly generated graphic

Text input field

For detailed information, see *Adding forms* in online Help.

6   In the **Form Properties** dialog, on the **Action** dialog:

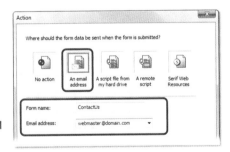

- Select **An e-mail address**.

- Type a name for your form. (This must not contain spaces or special characters.)

- Type the email address to which you want the site visitor's form data to be sent, e.g. webmaster@domain.com

- Click **Finish**.

7 To insert the form at default size, position the cursor where you want the form to appear and then click once.

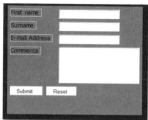

8 Preview your site to see what the form will look like when it's published.

Editing form layout

We're now going to adjust some of the elements on our form, so you might want to zoom in at this point.

There are a couple of things we want to change:

- We need to adjust the look of the form field labels.

- We're going to reposition the form **Submit** and **Reset** buttons.

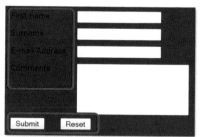

Luckily, WebPlus lets you move and edit form controls just as you would any other object. We'll demonstrate this now...

To move and align form buttons

1 Click on the **Submit** button and drag it into place under the 'Comments' text box, as illustrated.

2 Next, drag the **Reset** button into place below the **Submit** button.

3 Optional: If you need to increase the size of the form to accommodate the new button placement, simply select the grey form object and then click and drag a sizing handle.

4 Select the two buttons and the field text boxes.

5 On the **Align** tab, ensure that **Relative to: Selection** is displayed, and click the ⊩ **Left** align button.

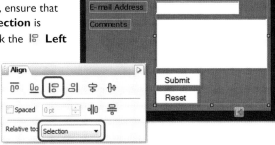

To right align form field labels

1 Select all four text labels.

2 On the **Align** tab ensure that **Relative to: Selection** is displayed, and click the **Right** align button.

Form labels are simply HTML text frames. This means that you can edit them in exactly the same way as an HTML frame that you place on the page. As we have a dark background, we're going to change the text colour so that it stands out.

To recolour label text

1 With the text frames still selected, on the **Swatches** tab, ensure that the Text fill button is selected.

For information on the various types of text frames available in WebPlus, and when to use them, see the online Help or the *Text* tutorial.

2 Click a colour swatch (we selected **Scheme Colour 5**).

The text is updated to match the new colour.

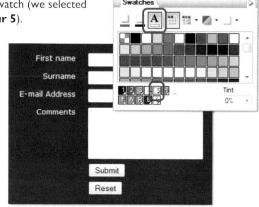

3 Preview your form in your web browser.

That's it! Once your form is published, visitors to your site can type their details directly into the text boxes provided. When they click **Submit**, the information is sent to the email address you specified when you created the form.

Blogs & Shout Boxes

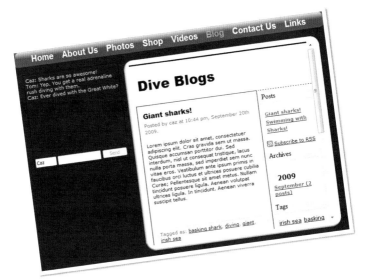

Add interactive blogs and shout boxes in this tutorial.

You'll learn how to:

- Configure, insert, and manage a blog.
- Format and insert a shout box.

Blogs & Shout Boxes

Blogs are online diaries. They allow you to frequently update articles and allow your visitors to post their own comments on your blog.

Shout boxes are more like web-based instant messengers. A shout box allows visitors to chat to each other in 'real time.'

While these objects might sound complicated to create, thanks to the WebPlus Smart objects, they're actually very easy! Over the next few steps, we'll add a blog and a shout box to our SCUBA diving website.

Serif Web Resources

For further information about creating a Serif Web Resource account, see the *Web Statistics* tutorial or *Using Smart objects* in online Help.

You'll find a version of the project file, **scuba.wpp**, in the **Workspace** folder. In a standard installation, you'll find this folder in the following location:

C:\Program Files\Serif\WebPlus\X4\Tutorials

To add a blog

1   On the **Site** tab, double-click the Blog page entry. The page opens in the workspace.

2   On the Web Objects toolbar, click the 🌐 **Smart Object Tool**. If necessary, log in to your account.

3   In the **Smart Objects** dialog, click **New...**

4   In the **Create Smart Object** dialog, select **Blog**, select a **Language** option, and click **OK**.

5   In the **Create Smart Object** dialog, in the **Style** pane on the right:

    • Type a name for the blog.

    • Adjust the appearance of the blog text (text colour, font style and size, and border colour and thickness).

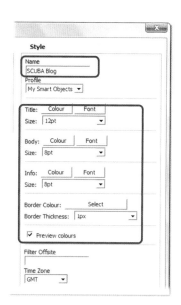

The **Blog Preview** pane updates as you make your changes.

6   Select your time zone from the drop-down list.

7   When you are happy with your blog settings, click **Create** to add the blog object to your **Smart Objects Library**.

Advanced blog options

You can control the appearance of your blog even further by selecting the following options:

- **Blogger Name**, **Description**, and **Photograph URL**: Use these boxes to provide additional 'profile' information about the blog and its author.

- **Visual Style**: To change the layout and presentation of your blog, select a preset visual style from the drop-down menu.

- **Alternative style sheet (CSS) URL**: To change the layout and presentation of your blog using a custom style sheet, type the URL of the style sheet *.css file into this box.

- **Layout**: To hide the header and/or sidebar of the blog, select the relevant check box(es).

- **Permalink**: Select to add a hyperlink beneath each blog article, allowing blog users to 'bookmark' an article and return to it later.

- **Article home link**: Select to add a link to the bottom of an article, allowing the user to navigate from an archived article back to the main blog.

- **Comments disabled**: Select to disable user commenting on your blog articles.

- **Blog RSS**: Select to include an RSS feed for the blog, allowing blog readers to keep up-to-date with the most recent blog articles.

- **Comments RSS**: Select to include an RSS feed for each blog article. This is a particularly useful for blogs containing very popular and 'active' articles, where blog users want to be informed of new comments that have been added to an article.

- **Archives**: Select to provide blog readers with access to monthly archives of blog articles.

- **Profile Info**: Select/clear this option to display/hide the blogger profile information.

- **Send Trackbacks**: Select to scan new blog articles for links to other blogs, then automatically notify the blog that it has been referenced (using standard 'trackback' and 'pingback' protocols).

- The **Social Bookmarks** section lets you provide blog users with the ability to submit articles to popular social bookmarking sites.

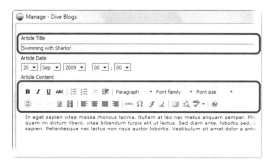

You can also add your blog as on offsite link. For more information on creating offsite links, see online Help.

8   Click **Insert** and then click on your page to add the blog.

9   Resize and position the blog object as required.

Managing blogs

Due to the nature of blogs, you'll probably want to manage these objects quite frequently. For example, to add new articles or even delete comments posted by site visitors (hopefully you won't need to do this too often!).

1   Click the 🏵 **Smart Object Tool**.

2   In the **Smart Objects Library**, select the blog then in the **Object Preview** pane click **Manage**.

3   In the **Manage Blog** dialog, several options are available.

To create a new blog article:

- Click **New**.

- Type your article title in the **Article Title** box.

- Type your article content in the main window. To format the text, use the toolbar controls.

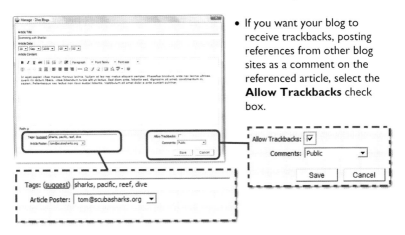

- If you want your blog to receive trackbacks, posting references from other blog sites as a comment on the referenced article, select the **Allow Trackbacks** check box.

- To categorize your article and allow blog users to search for similar articles of interest, type tag keywords into the **Tags** box. (For a list of suggested tags, click the **suggest** link.)

- Click **Save** to add the new article and return to the **Manage Blog** dialog.

  (You'll see your new article listed.)

To edit an existing article

- Select the article and click **Edit**. Make your changes and click **Save**.

WebPlus lets you control who is permitted to post comments to your blog articles is available in WebPlus. For example, you can:

- Prevent spam by using a CAPTCHA control.
- Restrict access by granting access to specific user groups.

For details, see *Access control* in online Help.

To delete an existing article

• Select the article and click **Delete**.

To edit article comments

• Select the article and click **Comments**. You can delete selected comments for an article, or clear all comments.

Shout boxes

Now let's add our shout box.

To add a shout box

1 In the **Smart Objects** dialog, click **New**.

2 In the **Create Smart Object** dialog, select **Shout Box** and click **OK**.

3 In the **Create New Shout Box** dialog:

   • Type a name for the shout box.

   • Use the controls to set the appearance of the shout box.

   • Click **Create** to add the shout box object to your library.

   • Click **Insert** and add the shout box to your page.

4 Preview the Smart objects on your new **Blog** page in your web browser.

   (Your page will not look like ours as you do not yet have any blog or shout box entries.)

Well, that concludes this project. If you want to take things further—allowing visitors to make online purchases from your web site—see the *E-Commerce* tutorial.

💡 You can also remove unwanted lines of text from your shout boxes.

To remove a shout box entry:

• In the **Manage Shout Box** dialog, click the word '**Delete**' next to the unwanted entry.

Access Control
& Mailing Lists

Access control lets you apply security to your website, either to restrict access to specific pages or to control user access to forums, blogs, and other Serif Web Resource features. In WebPlus, this is managed with a User List Smart object.

Another useful function of the User List Smart object is the ability to quickly create mailing lists.

In this tutorial, we'll show you how to:

- Set up access control.
- Configure, manage, and edit user groups.
- Suspend and block IP addresses and users.
- Create a mailing list.

This tutorial assumes that you have already registered for a **Serif Web Resources** account. If you are unsure how to do this, see the tutorial *Counters & Polls* or see online Help.

Access Control & Mailing Lists

The **User List** Smart object has two modes—*access control* and *mailing list.*

The access control mode allows you to easily control who can access the pages of your site, forums, blogs and other objects.

In mailing list mode, the User List object allows website visitors to sign up to newsletters, party confirmations, information requests, and many more. Lists can be controlled manually or by self-subscription.

To access the **Smart objects,** you need to log in to **Serif Web Resources**. If you don't have a valid username and password you must first create a Serif Web Resources account - see online Help or the *Counters & Polls* tutorial if you are unsure how to do this.

In this tutorial, we'll look at both modes, starting with access control.

Setting up access control

There are often times when you want to restrict access to certain pages within your site. Perhaps you have personal photo galleries that you only want friends and family to see, or you want to be able to monitor and control who uses your web forum. This is where the User List Smart object can help.

The **User List - Access Control** mode lets you apply security across your site (typically to specific pages of your site). In this exercise, we'll set up an **Access Control** Smart object to set security on our gallery page. Once we've done that, we can reuse the access control for our Forum in the next tutorial.

To set up access control

1 Start a new site, or alternatively, open the **scuba.wpp** file from the **Workspace** folder.

2 On the Web Objects toolbar, click the **Smart Object Tool** and log in to Serif Web Resources.

3 In the **Smart Objects** dialog, click **New.**

Workspace folder

In a standard installation, you'll find this folder in the following location:

C:\Program Files\Serif\WebPlus\X4\Tutorials\Workspace

4   In the **Create Smart Object** dialog, select the **User List** option and click **OK**.

5   In the **Create Smart Object** dialog, name your access control object.

- If you want to create an on-the-page user login, set the properties of the text, buttons, background, and border.

6   Click **Create**. Your new Smart object is listed in the Smart objects Library.

Style

Name	
SCUBA access control	
Profile	
My Smart Objects	
Title:	Colour	Font
Size:	8pt
Text and Labels:	Colour	Font
Size:	8pt
Buttons:	Colour	Font
Size:	8pt
Border Colour:	Select
Border Thickness:	2px
☑ Preview colours	

Adding users to the User List

Access control is based around a user list (i.e. a complete list of users who are registered on your site) and one or more user groups. Users can be added to the user list in two ways:

- Automatically - when a visitor registers or signs up on your site or forum.

- Manually - by adding a user in the **Manage** dialog. This is most useful when you want to restrict access to certain pages on your site and you have a dedicated list of people to add immediately.

As we are going to password protect our Gallery page, we'll start by manually adding some users to the list. Let's do this now.

To manually add a user to the User List

1   In the Smart object library, select your **User List - Access Control Mode** object and click **Manage**.

The **Users** section already contains one user—this is your Serif Web Resources login email address.

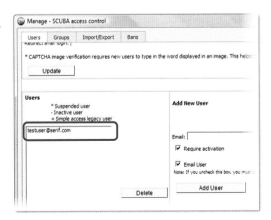

2   In the **Add New User** pane, type the user email address into the **Email** field.

3   Leave the default settings (recommended) and click **Add User**.

The user is added to the list and will receive a confirmation email with their login details.

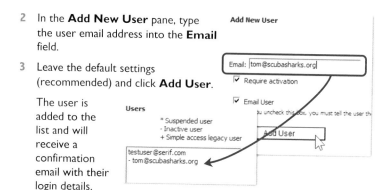

Add New User

Email: tom@scubasharks.org

☑ Require activation

☑ Email User

...ou uncheck this box, you must tell the user th...

Add User

Users

* Suspended user
- Inactive user
+ Simple access legacy user

testuser@serif.com
- tom@scubasharks.org

4   Add any other users.

💡 If you clear the **Require Activation** check box, the user will is automatically activated. They will be able to log in to the page with access control immediately.

Configuring access control

Now that we've created a new User List Access Control object, the next step is to configure our users and groups.

To create user groups

1   Click the 🏵 **Smart Object Tool**.

2   In the Smart Objects Library, select your **User List - Access Control Mode** object and click **Manage**.

3   In the **Manage** dialog, click the **Groups** tab.

Currently, the list of groups is empty. As we are going to set security on our gallery page, let's create a 'Gallery access' group.

4   Under **Create New Group**:

• Type '**Gallery access**' in the **Group Name** box.

• Ensure that the **Add new users on signup** option is cleared.

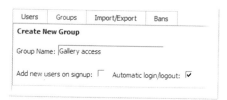

Users	Groups	Import/Export	Bans

Create New Group

Group Name: Gallery access

Add new users on signup: ☐   Automatic login/logout: ☑

- Click **Create Group**.

5 The **Group Management** panel displays the settings that you've just created. For now, click **Done**.

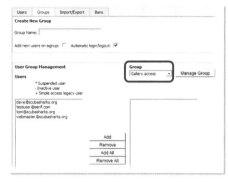

6 In the **User Group Management** pane, the **Group** drop-down list displays the name of your new group.

Notice that the group list is empty. Let's now add some users.

To manually add users to a group

1 On the **Groups** tab, ensure that your new group is selected.

2 To add users one at time:

- In the **Users** section, click to select a user name from the list.

- Click **Add**.

- or -

To add all users in the list, click **Add All**.

3 Once added to the group, the users appear in the group list.

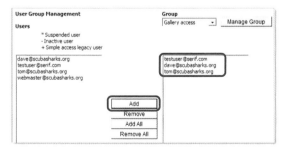

4 Click **Exit**.

Now that your 'Gallery access' control group is created, we can set up the page security on our photo gallery page. Let's do this now.

To apply page security

1 On the **Site** tab, double-click the **Gallery** page entry.

2 On the Pages context toolbar, click 🔒 **Page Security**.

3 In the **Page Properties** dialog, on the **Page Security** tab, select the **Protect page with password** option. Click **Change/Manage**.

4 In the **User Groups** dialog, select the 'Gallery access' group and click **OK**.

5 Back in the **Page Properties** dialog, the 'Gallery access' group in displayed next to the **Current User Group** field. Click **OK** to exit.

6 Click 🖥️ ▾ **Preview Site in {your browser of choice}** and click on the Gallery page. An **Authentication Required** dialog will appear. Log in to access the page.

You can use access control to apply security to other pages of your site, such as those containing confidential information. If you have several pages to protect, why not add an access control login object to your master page? For more details, see online Help.

Congratulations! You've successfully created an access control user list and used it to protect your page.

Suspending and banning users

Your **User List - Access Control** object can be used by any smart object that requires a user list. In the next tutorial, we will create a forum that uses our access control object. This will allow users to automatically sign up to the site forum. However, this means that you'll need to know how to protect your site from unwanted users.

In the **Manage** dialog, the **User Control** section allows you to suspend users temporarily for breaking site rules (for example, for posting defamatory statements on a hosted public forums).

If more drastic action is required, a user's IP address can be banned from accessing the forum. As a last resort, even the ISP or organization to which the owner of the email address belongs can be banned.

As a general rule, the latter option is not recommended. However, it may sometimes be necessary to prevent institutional malpractice such as professional spamming.

To suspend a user

1   Log in to Serif Web Resources.

2   In the Smart Objects Library, select your User List - Access Control object, then click **Manage**.

3   In the **Manage** dialog, click the **Bans** tab.

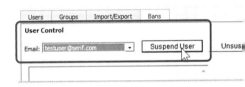

4   Under **User Control**, select a user from the **Email** drop-down list.

5   Click **Suspend User**.

On the **Users** tab, in the **Users** list, suspended users are indicated with an asterisk.

The next time the user tries to log on, the message "Your account has been suspended" is displayed.

To reactivate a suspended user

•   Select the user and, on the **Bans** tab, click **Unsuspend User**.

To ban a user by IP address

1   Follow steps 1 to 2 of the previous section, 'To suspend a user'.

2   In the **Ban User's** drop-down list, select **IP address**.

3   Click **Ban**.

Banning an ISP or organization can result in innocent visitors to your site also being banned. It is recommended that you only apply an ISP ban as a last measure.

Note that banning a single ISP from America Online may also affect other users.

To ban a user by ISP or organization

1   Follow steps 1 to 2 of the previous section, 'To suspend a user'.

2   Click the **Lookup User** button.

Serif Web Resources locates the user's ISP/organization network address and displays it in the scrolling window.

As the **Lookup User** function relies upon external websites (those responsible for allocating IP addresses), it may sometimes fail due to timing out.

3   In the **Ban User's** drop-down list, select **ISP/organization**.

4   Click **Ban**.

If a user's IP address, ISP, or organization is banned, it is listed in an **Unban** drop-down list. The entry will also include the date the address was banned.

This allows you to review current bans and reverse them if the user, IP address, or organization is no longer considered suspect.

In this tutorial, we've shown you how to set up an access control user list object, which we will use in the next tutorial, *Forums*. However, the User List object has another function—mailing lists.

Mailing Lists

With a mailing list you can have website visitors sign up to newsletters, party confirmations, information requests, and so on. The lists can be controlled manually or by self-subscription.

All mailing lists begin life as a User List in Access Control mode. As such, to create a new mailing list object, follow the steps in the *To set up access control* section.

Next, we need to convert the object to a mailing list.

To create a mailing list

1　Click the 🔷 **Smart Object Tool**.

2　In the Smart Objects Library, select your **User List - Access Control Mode** object and click **Manage**.

3　On the **Users** tab, in the **Signup and Login** drop-down list, select **Mailing List Mode** and then click **Update**.

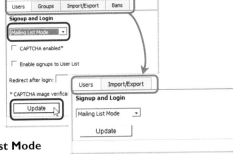

Notice that the dialog tabs change to only those that are need to create and manage a mailing list.

To manually add users

1　In the **Add New User** pane, type the user email address into the **Email** field.

2　Leave the default settings (recommended) and click **Add User.**

The user is added to the list and will receive a confirmation email and/or activation details.

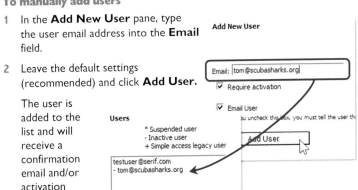

3   Add any other users.

To add a mailing list signup to a site page

1   Open the site master page and click the 🏵 **Smart Object Tool**.

2   Locate your User List - Mailing List object in the Library pane, click to select it and then, click **Insert**.

3   Click to insert the mailing list signup object on the page.

4   **Optional step:** Add a text frame inviting your viewers to sign up to the mailing list.

To manage a mailing list

1   Log in to Serif Web Resources.

2   In the Smart Objects Library, select your User List - Mailing List object, then click **Manage**.

The **Manage** dialog displays a list of all the email addresses collected:

- To delete an individual email address, click **Delete**.

- Import and/or Export a list of users from the **Import/Export** tab.

    (This will automatically give everyone on the list a username they can use to log into your site.)

 Importing Lists

A large number of users can be quickly added to your site by importing a CSV file containing a list of email addresses only. Such a list can be exported from many email clients and created with various spreadsheet programs.

Congratulations! You can now protect your site pages and have the ability to contact your fan base. The rest is up to you. Now that you know how to create user lists, why not try the *Forum* tutorial. Have fun!

Forums

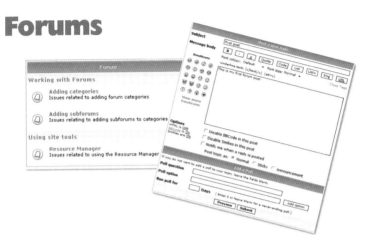

Use the forum Smart object to host interactive discussions on your websites.

In this tutorial you'll learn how to:

- Create a forum—on a page of your website, or as an offsite link.

- Configure, manage, and edit forums.

- Sign up and post to a forum.

- Add a forum moderator group.

- Create and edit forum user ranks.

This tutorial assumes that you have already completed the *Access Control & Mailing Lists* tutorial.

Forums

A forum allows visitors to your website to interact, hold discussions, and 'post' general comments and questions. Not only do forums allow you to gather feedback from the people who visit your site, they also provide a place for visitors to go to learn more about your products and services, or to discuss a common topic of interest.

The following steps show you how to add the forum as an offsite link.

Creating a forum

Once you have set up access control (see the *Access Control & Mailing List* tutorial), you can create your forum.

> **⚠ Access Control**
>
> To add a forum Smart object, you must first create an Access Control **User List**. See the *Access Control & Mailing List* tutorial or online Help for more information.
>
> Once you have created a forum, you cannot change its main forum name, or the Access Control object associated with it.

To create a forum

1   On the Web Objects toolbar, click the 🌐 **Smart Objects Tool**. If necessary, log in to your account.

2   In the **Smart Objects** dialog, click **New...**

3   In the **Create Smart Object** dialog, select the **Forum object** and click **OK**.

4   In the next dialog:

  • Name your forum.

  • Type a brief description of the forum.

  • In the **Access Control** drop-down list, select the Access Control object you created in the previous section.

  • Select your Time Zone from the drop-down list.

  • Click **Create**.

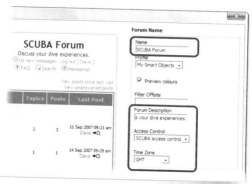

Your forum is added to the Smart objects Library and ready to be added to your site.

Due to the way forums are formatted, it is generally advised to add them as an offsite link. We'll do this now.

To add a forum as an offsite link

1 Once you have created your forum, click **Exit** to log out of Serif Web Resources.

2 On the **Site** tab, in the 🗋 ▾ **Add** drop-down list, click **New Offsite Link...**

3 In the **Offsite Link** dialog, select **Smart Object** and click the **None** button.

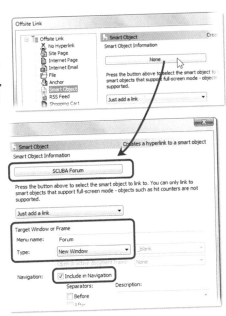

4 In the Smart Objects Library, select your forum and click **Select**.

5 Name your forum menu item and choose **New Window** in the **Type:** drop-down list. Select the **Include in Navigation** check box.

6 Click **OK**.

Due to the nature of forums, we recommend that you always add them as an offsite link. However, you can also add them to a site page just like any other Smart object.

To add a forum to a page

1 With the forum selected in the Smart Objects Library, click **Insert**.

2 Click and drag on your page to set the size of the object.

The offsite link is added to the **Site** tab.

On your web page, a new button is added to the navigation bar.

Configuring and managing the forum

You have now created everything you need to get your forum up and running—your forum will automatically create its own access control group within your access control object. However, there are a few configuration tasks you should know about before you go 'live' with your site.

If you take a look at the preview of your forum Smart object, you'll see the first main section is titled 'Test category 1,' with 'Test Forum 1' listed beneath it. These are the default settings that are automatically added to every new forum.

Category ⟶

Subforum ⟶

Each forum object can have multiple categories, each of which can also have multiple 'subforums.'

The **Manage Forum** dialog lets you edit the default test category and its subforum, and create additional categories and subforums.

You can also edit forum and subforum descriptions, add a moderator group, set permissions, change the style (theme) of the forum, add and rank users, and set user permissions.

Setting forum permissions

The **Manage Forum** dialog also includes a **Forum Privacy** section. Here, you can set permissions to determine if non-registered visitors to your site can read your forums.

- If you want non-registered visitors to be able to read your forums, set permissions to **Publicly readable**.
- If you only want registered visitors to view your forums, set permissions to **Private**.

In the next section, we'll do the following:

- Edit the default category and its subforum.
- Add a new forum to the updated category.
- Add a second category and subforum.
- Change the forum theme.

To edit the default category and subforum

1   In the Smart Objects Library, select your forum and then, click **Manage**.

2   In the **Manage Forum** dialog, in the **Forum Management** section, replace the default **Category Name** text with your own category name.

Click **Update Category**.

3   Type your new **Forum Name** and **Forum Description**.

Click **Update Forum**.

Forum Management

To edit the name of a category or forum, change its old name and press enter, or

Category Name	
Working with Forums	Update Category

Forum Name	Forum Description
Adding categories	Issues related to adding forum categories
	Moderated By Group
	No moderation ▼

To add a new subforum to an existing category

1   In the **Add New Forum** section, type a name and description for your new subforum.

2   In the **Forum Category** drop-down list, select the category to which you want to add the new subforum (you will only see one category listed.)

Add New Forum:

Forum Name	Forum Description
Adding subforums	Issues related to adding subforums to categories

Forum Category	
Working with Forums ▼	Add Forum

3   Click **Add Forum**.

4   Scroll back to the **Forum Management** section to see your updated category name with its two subforums listed beneath it.

Let's now add a second category and subforum to our main forum.

To add a new category and subforum

1   In the **Add New Category** section, type the name for your new category and click **Add Category**.

2   In the **Add New Forum** section, type a name and description for your new subforum.

3   In the **Forum Category** drop-down list, you'll now see two categories listed. Select the new category you created in the previous step.

4   Click **Add Forum**.

In the **Forum Management** section, you will see your new category and its subforum listed beneath it.

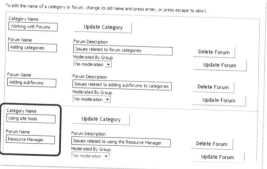

Finally, let's change the general appearance of the main forum object by applying a different theme.

To change a forum theme

1   In the **Manage Forum** dialog, in the **Forum Themes** section, select a theme from the drop-down list and then click **Update Theme**.

2   Click **Exit** to close the **Manage Forum** dialog and return to the **Smart Objects** dialog.

3   Click **Exit** to return to the WebPlus workspace and preview your forum.

In the previous tutorial, *Access Control & Mailing Lists*, you configured your **User List-Access Control** object. Let's now see how it works together with the forum Smart object.

Signing in to access control and posting to the forum

You'll now assume the role of a visitor to your website. You'll sign in to access control and then post a new topic to the forum.

For this section, use a different email account to the one you used to sign up for Serif Web Resources. If you don't have an alternate email address, it's very easy to set one up (you can create free email accounts at Yahoo, Hotmail, AOL, and many other providers' sites).

To sign in to the Access Control object

1   On the Standard toolbar, in the 🖳 ▾ **Preview Site** drop-down list, click **Preview Site in {browser of choice}**.

2   If you have used an offsite link, click the relevant navigation bar button, and then click **Register** at the top of the forum page.

3 Your browser is redirected to a **Forum Account - Sign up** page.

Complete the details as requested and then click **Signup**.

The email address you specified on the Signup page will receive an email with the subject **Account Activation (Forum Account)**.

4 Click the link in the email to activate your account.

5 If you have used an offsite link, click **Login** at the top of the forum page.

6 Click on a subforum, and then click the **Post new topic** button.

7 Type your subject and message body into the text boxes and then click **Submit**.

You can now choose to view your message or return to the **Forum Index** page, which now indicates that a post has been created.

Adding a moderator group

The forum moderator is the person, or group, who monitors the forum—usually on a daily basis. The moderator's role is to prevent forum users from posting offensive messages, or messages that are not related to the forum topic.

Moderators can edit and delete posts, and also delete, lock, unlock, split, and move topics in the forum. You can take on this role yourself, or you can assign someone else the position. Either way, if you want to assign a moderator to your forum, you will need to do the following:

- Create a new group.
- Add a user to the group.
- Assign the group to the forum Smart object.
- Designate the group as the forum moderator.

To create and assign a moderator group

1 Log in to Serif Web Resources.

2 In the Smart Objects Library, select your User List-Access Control object and click **Manage**.

3 In the **Manage** dialog, under **Create New Group**:

- Click the **Group** tab.

- In the **Group Name** text box, type a name for your moderator group.

- In the **Group Smart Object** drop-down list, select your forum Smart object.

- Do not select the **Add new users on signup** check box.

- If you are adding your forum to a page of your site, you can also select **Automatic login/logout**.

  For an offsite link, you can leave this check box clear.

- Click **Create Group**.

- Click **Done** in the Group Management pane to return to the main dialog.

You can now add users to your Moderator group.

4   In the **User Group Management** section:

- In the **Group** drop-down list, select the Forum Moderator group.

- In the **Users** list, click a user.

Because you signed up to the forum as a new user with an alternate email address, you will see several users in this list.

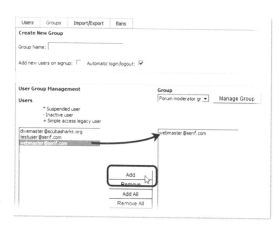

- Click **Add** to add the selected user to the Moderator group.

- Click **Manage Group**.

The **Manage Access Control** dialog displays your updated group properties and user.

- Click **Done** and then **Exit** to return to the object Library.

- In the **Smart Objects Library**, select your forum object and click **Manage**.

5 In the **Manage Forum** dialog, under **Forum Management**:

- Locate the subforum to which you want to add a moderator.

- In the **Moderated By Group** drop-down list, select your forum moderator group.

- Click **Update Forum**.
- Click **Exit** to close the Smart Object Library.

When your site is published, members of the moderator group will be able to click a link (located in the lower right corner of the subforum and topic pages) to open the **Moderator Control Panel**.

In the **Moderator Control Panel**, the moderator can delete, move, lock, unlock, and split forum topics.

You **can** post new topics in this forum
You **can** reply to topics in this forum
You **can** edit your posts in this forum
You **can** delete your posts in this forum
You **can** vote in polls in this forum
You **can** moderate this forum

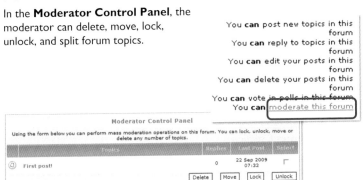

Creating, editing, and assigning user ranks

A **rank** is a title that appears in each user's profile, and next to their screenname when they post to a forum.

You can use ranks to indicate something about a member or group of members. For example, to indicate that certain users have a special status, or to show how active they are on the forum, and so on.

There are two types of ranks, **normal ranks** and **special ranks**.

- Normal ranks are granted to all users based on their forum post count.
- Special ranks are granted to specific users in the **Rank User** section of the dialog.

To create a new normal rank

1   Log in to Serif Web Resources.

2   In the Smart Objects Library, select your forum object and click **Manage**.

3   In the **Manage** dialog, scroll to the **User Rank Management** section.

4   In the **Add New Rank** section, in the **Rank Title** box, type a name for the new rank.

5   In the **Min. Posts** box, type the minimum number of posts users must have created in order to achieve this rank.

For example, in our illustration, a user would be granted the **Power User** rank only after creating 100 forum posts.

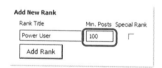

6   Click **Add Rank**.

The new rank is added to the rank list.

To create a new special rank

1   In the **Manage Forum** dialog, scroll to the **User Rank Management** section.

2   In the **Add New Rank** section, in the **Rank Title** box, type the name for the new rank.

3   Leave the **Min. Posts** box empty and select the **Special Rank** check box.

4 Click **Add Rank**.

Again, the new rank is added to the rank list.

To assign a special rank to a user

In the **Rank User** section:

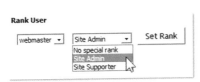

- Select a user from the first drop-down list .

- Select the special rank from the second drop-down list.

- Click **Set Rank**.

That's it! You should now have all of the tools you need to create and maintain a forum. For information on suspending and banning users, see the *Access Control & Mailing List* tutorial.

Further Development

This section provides more advanced exercises to help you develop your site by including e-commerce functionality, iFrames, and database-merged fields.

Image Catalogue

In this tutorial, we'll use WebPlus's **database merge** functionality to showcase a collection of artwork.

You'll learn how to:

- Create a photo database.
- Insert a repeating area on the page.
- Open and edit a database.
- Add hyperlinks providing site visitors with access to additional information about an image.
- Merge and publish data.

Adding an Image Catalogue

In this exercise we'll create an image catalogue for a graphic artist's website. We'll create a photo data source from a folder of images, and merge the data into a repeating area on our page. We'll then customize the repeating area, and edit the data to create an attractive catalogue of artwork samples. We'll complete the following steps:

- Create a photo database from a folder of images.

- Insert repeating areas for the data.

- Insert placeholders into repeating areas.

> The Photo Data Source function handles image files in any standard format.

- Open and edit the database.

- Merge and publish the data.

- Link summary and main pages for each record, using anchors and hyperlinks.

- Link merged page names to image and HTML file names.

I: Preparing the site

In preparation for inserting our image catalogue, we did the following:

1   We created a ⬜ new blank site, adding a banner and company details to the top of the master page.

2   On the **Site** tab, we added a ⊞ new blank page and named it **Draft layout**.

3   On our **Draft layout** page, we created a mockup of the page layout we wanted to achieve.

    (You can do this in WebPlus, or with paper and pencil.)

If you create your draft layout in WebPlus, you'll need to either delete this page before you publish your site, or clear its check box in the **Publish to Web** dialog (see section 7, *Merging and publishing the site*, step 5.).

2: Creating the database

We're now ready to create our photo database. You can use a collection of any images for this exercise, but before completing the following steps, you'll need to save all of the images to the same folder on your computer.

To create a photo database

1   On the **View** toolbar, select **Toolbars**, then click **Database Merge**. (This toolbar is hidden by default.)

2   On the Database Merge toolbar, click ⑧ **Create photo database**.

3   In the **Photo Data Source Wizard**, click **Browse**, then locate the source folder containing the images you want to database. (All images must be contained in the same folder.) Select the folder and click **OK**.

4   Click **Next**.

5   If required, edit the file name of the database to be created, or accept the default name.

Click **Next**.

6 The Wizard displays a list of image files found in the designated source folder.

   Initially, all images are checked for inclusion in the database. If required, you can clear check boxes to exclude specific images.

   Click **Next**.

7 The Wizard displays a list of Exif data fields that may be associated with your images.

   In this exercise, we don't want to include this information so click **Select None** to clear all of the check boxes.

8 Click **Finish**.

   WebPlus builds the database.

💡 Keen photographers may find the Exif data useful: Each database record created will consist of a path name for the photo, plus fields containing additional Exif data (date and time, equipment, software, etc.) that may have been automatically stored with the original file.

3: Creating the repeating area

Now that we have created our photo database, we can associate it with a **repeating area** on a web page. Inside this repeating area, we can then insert our database picture and text fields, along with any other elements that we want to repeat on the page (in this case, a shape).

To create the repeating area

1 On the Database toolbar, click 📇 **Insert Repeating Area**.

2   In the **Choose merge database** dialog, click **Browse**, then browse to and select the database created in the previous section.

3   Click **OK**.

The **Repeating Area Tile Setup** dialog lets you choose the layout required for your page.

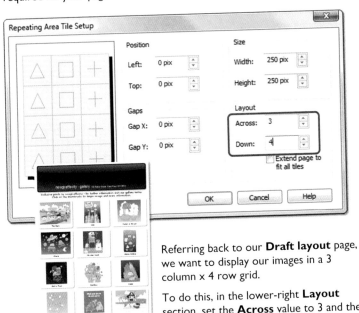

Referring back to our **Draft layout** page, we want to display our images in a 3 column x 4 row grid.

To do this, in the lower-right **Layout** section, set the **Across** value to 3 and the **Down** value to 4.

4   Click **OK** to close the dialog.

Setting up the repeating area

You can set precise properties for the repeating area in the dialog, or close the dialog and then click and drag to set the repeating area's size and shape directly on the page.

5   On your page, WebPlus creates a placeholder for the first cell of the repeating area.

If required, you can:

• Move the repeating area cell by clicking and dragging it.

• Resize the repeating area cell by dragging its border handles.

We can now add the objects that we want to display in each repeating area on the page. We'll start by creating a simple QuickShape, which we'll use as a 'frame' for each image.

6   On the ☐ ▾ QuickShapes flyout, click the **QuickRectangle** and then click and drag on the page to create a rectangle. Drag the left node down to round the corners.

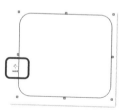

• On the **Swatches** tab, apply a white fill.

• On the **Line** tab, in the line style drop-down list, select **None**.

7   On the ⌂ ▾ Effects flyout, click *fx* **Filter Effects**.

8   In the **Filter Effects** dialog, select the **Drop Shadow** check box and then set the following values:

  • **Opacity** 36;

  • **Blur** 3.75;

  • **Distance** 3.75;

  • **Angle** 135

  • Clear the **Scale with object** check box.

  Click **OK**.

Drop Shadow

Blend Mode:	Multiply ▾	
Opacity:	△	36
Blur:	△	3.75 pt
Intensity:	△	0
Colour:	▾	
Lock:	Centre ▾	
Scale X:		100
Shear Y:		0
Scale Y:		100
Shear X:		0
Distance:	△	3.75 pt

Angle: 135

☐ Scale with object

OK   Canc

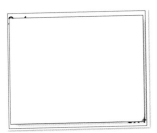

9   Drag the rectangle into the repeating area, resizing it so that it just fits inside.

    Now let's add our database fields to the repeating area.

10 On the Database Merge toolbar, click 🖼 **Insert Picture Field**.

11 In the **Insert Picture Field** dialog, in the **Fields** list, you'll see **Path Name** selected by default. Click **Insert** to insert this field, and then click **Close**.

Insert Picture Field

Click 'Insert' to add the selected field to your site

Fields:
Path Name

☑ Show only picture fields

Insert   Close

WebPlus adds the {**MM:Path Name**} placeholder to your page at default size.

12 Drag the placeholder into the repeating area and resize it so that it fits inside the rectangle shape. Leave some space underneath to add the image title.

4: Editing the database

Next, we'll edit our database, creating additional text fields for the image titles and descriptions.

To edit the data source

1 On your web page, click to select the border of the repeating area placeholder (make sure you select the repeating area itself and not the {**MM:Path Name**} placeholder).

On the Database Merge toolbar, click ▦ **Edit Database**. (You can also click **Edit Database** on the context toolbar.)

2 In the **Choose merge database** dialog, your database file name is displayed in the **Data source** text box. Click **Edit**.

3 In the **Merge List** dialog, click **Edit**.

🔖 The **Merge List** dialog is used to customize the data to be merged by including or excluding specific records, filtering the records, or editing the data.

💡 If you can't see a thumbnail preview in the **Edit Database** dialog, click in the **Path Name** field. The image associated with the record will be displayed.

4   In the **Edit Database** dialog, click **Customize**.

5   In the **Customize Database** dialog, click **Insert**.

6   In the **Field Name** dialog, type 'Image Name' and click **OK**.

7   Repeat steps 5 and 6 to add a second text field. Name this field 'Description'.

8   Click **OK** to close the **Customize Database** dialog.

In the **Edit Database** dialog, your new fields are added to the record details.

9   Type the name and description of your first image directly into the text boxes, then click the right arrow button to move to the next record.

10 Repeat step 9 to add names and descriptions for the remaining images, then click **OK** to close the dialog.

11 Click **OK** to close the **Choose merge database** dialog.

12 On the Database Merge toolbar, click 🎎 **Insert Text Field**.

In the **Insert Text Field** dialog, in the **Fields** list, select **Image Name**.

13 Click **Insert** to insert this field, and then click **Close**.

WebPlus adds the **{MM:Image Name}** placeholder to your page at default size.

14 Drag this new placeholder into position under the image placeholder.

Centre align the text by clicking ≡ **Align Centre** on the Text context toolbar.

15 Click 🖫 **Save** to save your work.

5: Merging data into the repeating area

Now that we have selected which records to merge (that is, we have created our **merge list**), and inserted our placeholders, we're ready to merge the database content to a temporary website and preview the results of our work.

To merge the repeating area

1 On the Database Merge toolbar, click 📄 **Merge to New Site** (or click 📄 on the context toolbar).

WebPlus generates a new website (adding the suffix '**_merge1**' to the file name) in a separate window, replicating the repeating area as many times as there are records in the database, and replacing the placeholders with the relevant database fields.

The layout uses the grid arrangement you specified (3 x 4 in our example), with each unique cell including data from a single record, following the order of records in the merge list.

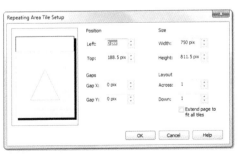 In our example, all of our 12 records fit on a single page. However, WebPlus will insert new pages as needed to include all records in the database.

2   **Optional:** To adjust display properties such as picture scaling and alignment for any individual picture frame, right-click the frame and click **Frame Properties...**

Note that the original website remains open in its own window. Don't forget to save it in case you need to repeat the merge process with another data set!

If you're not happy with the resulting merged website, return to the original site, make adjustments, and repeat the merge process.

3   When you're happy with your page layout, close the merged site window and return to your original site.

6: Adding a details page, anchor, and hyperlink

In this final section, we'll add some interactivity to our site. We want site visitors to be able to click on an image thumbnail to open a new page containing a larger version of the image, and a detailed description.

To add the details page

1   On the **Site** tab, click 🗋 **Add** to add a new blank page to your site. In the **Insert** dialog, accept the default page settings for now.

2   On the Database Merge toolbar, click 🔁 **Insert Repeating Area**.

3   In the **Choose merge database** dialog, click **Browse**. Select your image database and click **OK**.

4   In the **Repeating Area Tile Setup** dialog, choose a 1 column x 1 row grid layout. Click **OK**.

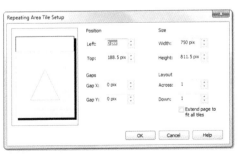

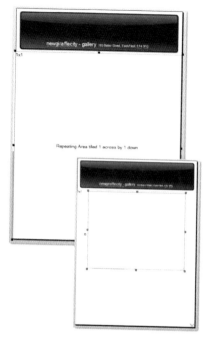

5 Resize the repeating area so that it fills your page.

6 Copy the QuickRectangle from your Home page, and then paste the shape onto your new page.

7 Resize the shape and position it at the top of the repeating area. Leave enough space at the bottom of the page for the Description text field.

8 On the Database Merge toolbar, click ▣ **Insert Picture Field**.

9 In the **Insert Picture Field** dialog, click **Insert** to add the **Path Name** field, and then click **Close**.

10 Drag the {**MM:Path Name**} placeholder into the repeating area, resizing it so that it fits inside the rectangle. Leave some space underneath to add the image title.

11 On the Database Merge toolbar, click ♛ **Insert Text Field**.

12 In the **Insert Text Field** dialog, select **Image Name**, click **Insert**, and then click **Close**.

Drag the {**MM:Image Name**} placeholder into position under the image placeholder.

13 Repeat steps 11 and 12 to add the **{MM:Description}** placeholder to the bottom of the page.

14 Select each text field placeholder in turn, and then use the controls on the Text context toolbar to apply formatting as required.

For example, for our Description field, we applied 10 pt Verdana, and left-aligned the text.

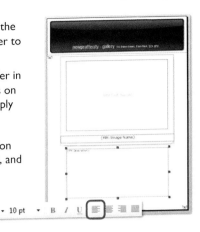

15 On the **Site** tab, right-click your new page and click **Page Properties**.

- In the **Page Properties** dialog, to the right of the **Page name** text box, click 🈴 **Insert Merge Field**.

- In the **Insert Text Field** dialog, select **Image Name** and click **Insert**.

On the **Site** tab, you'll see the page name is updated with the **{MM:Image Name}** placeholder text. (You'll see why we did this when we merge the data.)

We've finished placing the required elements into our repeating areas. Now all we have to do is link the thumbnail images on the Home page to the larger images and descriptions on the **{MM:Image Name}** page. We'll use an anchor and a hyperlink for this.

To add the anchor

1 On the **{MM:Image Name}** site page, select the large **{MM:Path Name}** placeholder.

2 On the Tools toolbar, on the  **Hyperlinks** flyout, click ⚓ **Anchor**.

3 In the **Anchor** dialog, type a name for the anchor—we named ours BigPic.

4 Click **OK**.

To add the hyperlink

1 Open the Home page in the workspace and select the thumbnail **{MM:Path Name}** placeholder.

2 On the Tools toolbar, on the Hyperlinks flyout, click 🌐 **Hyperlink**.

3 In the **Hyperlinks** dialog, in the left tree view, click **Anchor**.

4 To the right of the list, in the **Anchor** section of the dialog:

   • In the **Page name** drop-down list, select the **{MM:Image Name}** page.

   • In the **Anchor** list, select the anchor you created in the previous section.

   • In the database record drop-down link, select **Same record as origin of link**.

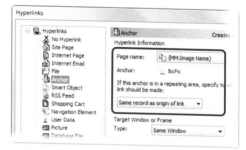

5 Click **OK**.

6 Save your file.

When you save a website, WebPlus 'remembers' the current data source and reopens it automatically the next time you open the site—so as long as you're using the same source, you won't need to reopen it yourself.

7: Merging and publishing the site

Our site is finished, but before we can publish it, we need to repeat the merge process to include the changes we have made to our database and site structure.

To merge and publish the data

1   On the Database Merge toolbar, click **Merge to New Site** (or click on the context toolbar).

WebPlus generates a new website (adding the suffix '**_merge2**' to the file name) in a separate window, creating a **{MM:Image Name}** page for each record in the database.

You'll see these pages listed on the **Site** tab.

You'll also see that WebPlus has replaced the page name placeholder text with the text found in each **Image Name** field. If we had not replaced the default page name with the **{MM:Image Name}** placeholder, all of these pages would have been named Page 3.

2   Double-click on one of your generated pages to preview it.

3   **Optional**: To adjust picture scaling and alignment for any individual picture frame, right-click the frame and click **Frame Properties...**

When you're happy with your page layout, you're ready to publish your website.

4   On the Standard toolbar, click **Publish to Disk**, or **Publish to Web**.

5 In the **Publish** dialog, select all the pages of your site, except for the **Draft Layout** page created in section 1, *Preparing the site*.

For details on the choosing your publishing options, see the online Help or the *Previewing & Publishing* tutorial.

6 Choose your publishing options as required, and then click **OK**.

7 View your site in your web browser.

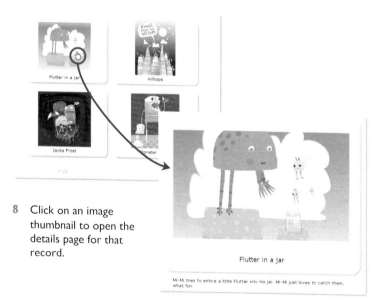

8 Click on an image thumbnail to open the details page for that record.

Flutter in a jar

Mi-Mi tries to entice a little Flutter into his jar. Mi-Mi just loves to catch them, what fun.

We've used a simple example for our example, but of course you can create more elaborate sites, adding multiple database fields to the details page, even additional images if required.

Note also that WebPlus lets you present other types of content—product lists, contact lists, e-commerce data, and so on, from a variety of data sources. For more details, see online Help.

E-commerce

If you've ever bought anything online, you'll know how simple the process can be as a buyer. But how difficult is it to set up your own e-store? Fortunately with WebPlus, the process simple. Over the next few pages, we'll show you how by creating a page to sell photographic prints.

In this project, you'll learn how to:

- Configure your e-commerce shopping cart provider. Our example uses PayPal© as our shopping cart provider. You may decide to use a different provider, depending on your needs and the product(s) you want to sell on your site.

- Add an e-commerce form and functionality to your site.

E-commerce

In the following sections, we'll configure a shopping cart provider, and insert and configure an e-commerce form.

1: Choosing a Shopping Cart Provider

You've made the decision to sell your products over the Internet and have created a site that will attract your target market.

But how do you accept and process payments from your customers?

Any website that supports e-commerce activity will typically make use of a shopping cart system and a payment processing system. If you've ever bought anything online, you will already be familiar with this concept.

There are many third-party shopping cart providers that can be used. Each provider offers the same basic features—product catalogue, 'running' customer basket, 'buy it now' option, secure payment information capture and checkout, and so on.

💡 Some cart providers offer additional features and depending on your needs, these may or may not be important to you.

Use the provider's Help pages to find out more about unique shopping cart features.

With WebPlus, you can choose one of our selected providers, all of which offer a good range of features.

In this project, we've chosen PayPal© as the provider most suited to sell some photo prints. We'll now step you through the signup and configuration process.

To setup and configure a PayPal shopping cart

1 On the Web Objects toolbar, on the E-commerce flyout, click the
   🖼 **Configure E-commerce** button.

2 In the **E-commerce Configuration** dialog, select the **PayPal** option and choose one of the following options:

   • If you already have a PayPal account, click **Next**.

   • If you don't have an account, click **Sign Up Now**. The PayPal site opens in your browser. Follow the instructions provided to register and set up an account. When you have finished, return to WebPlus.

3 In the **PayPal Configuration** dialog:

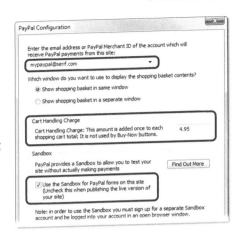

- Type the email address where you want to receive notification about payments received.

- Set the **Cart Handling Charge**, i.e. your default overall shipping charge.

- Optional step (recommended): If you want to use PayPal's **Sandbox**, a test tool for trying out your shopping cart before going live, select this option.

To use the Sandbox, you must set up a separate test account (in addition to your live PayPal login) through PayPal's Developer Central site. Click **Find Out More** to do this.

4 Click **Finish**.

Once you've configured your shopping cart, you're ready to insert an e-commerce object.

2: Inserting e-commerce objects

WebPlus provides Wizards to help you create e-commerce objects by completing a series of dialogs. You can add your e-commerce objects as a form or link, depending on the characteristics of the item(s) you are selling.

In our example, we'll add a form since it offers more flexibility and allows for some user interactivity. You can either use the **Workspace** files provided or use your own.

To open the Workspace file

1 On the Standard toolbar, click 📂 **Open**.

2 Navigate to the **Workspace** folder and click to select the **scuba.wpp** project file. In a typical installation, this folder is found in:

C:\Program Files\Serif\WebPlus\X4\Tutorials

3 Click **Yes** in the dialog to open as a new, untitled site.

4 Click **File > Save As...** and save your new file under a new name.

Our site uses **empty frames** as image placeholders. This makes it very easy to create thumbnails of our e-commerce objects and means that we can replace images very easily while retaining aspect ratio. For more information on using frames, se the *Pictures* tutorial.

To add an object image and title

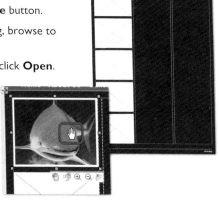

1 On the **Site** tab, double-click the **Shop** page entry to display the page.

2 Click to select the first picture frame, then click the 🖋 **Replace Picture** button.

3 In the **Import Picture** dialog, browse to your **Workspace** folder.

4 Select the **shark.jpg** file and click **Open**.

The picture is added to the frame and scaled to maximum-fit by default.

5 To reposition the picture inside the frame, click 🖐 **Pan**, and then click and drag on the picture with the 🖐 **Pan** cursor.

6 On the Standard Objects toolbar, In the Text frames flyout, click the 📄 **HTML Text Frame Tool**.

7 Click and drag on the page next to the image to place an HTML frame approximately 470 pix x 30 pix, between the empty column layout guides.

8 In the Text context toolbar, select the Heading 3 style from the drop-down list.

Heading 3   ▾ Verdana

9 Click in the text frame and type 'Reef shark print'.

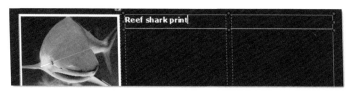

We are now ready to add our e-commerce details for this print.

To insert a PayPal form

1   On the Web Objects toolbar, on the E-commerce flyout, click the
    ⑤ Insert an E-commerce object button.

2   In the **Add PayPal Object** dialog:

    • Select the email address that is to receive the payment information.

    • WebPlus assumes that the email address set during shopping cart
      configuration is used. If you want to use a different address—for
      example, the address you specified when you set up your Sandbox,
      clear the **Use the site default address** box and select a different address to override the site default.

    PayPal Account information
    Choose the PayPal account which will receive this payment:
    ☐ Use the site default account
    sandbox@serif.com

    💡 For information on the differences
    between forms and links and why you might
    choose one over the other, see *Inserting an
    e-commerce object* in online Help.

    • Select the **Add to Shopping Cart Form** option.

    • Click **Next**.

3   In the **Button Image** dialog:

    • Select the **Use a standard image** option.

    • Select the image of your choice—we chose the first one.

    • Ensure that the **Embed image file in site** option is selected.

    • Click **Next**.

Button Image

Choose the image you would like to use for your button:

◯ Use a standard text button   Text: Add To Cart

◉ Use a standard image

    PayPal
    ADD TO CART

    PayPal
    ADD ITEM TO CART

    ADD TO CART

    Add to Cart

4 In the **Item Details** dialog, enter the following information:

- **Item Name:** The name of the item for sale. Try to make this descriptive as it will appear as the item description on the invoice produced by the cart. We typed 'Reef shark print'—the title of the photograph displayed in the first picture frame.

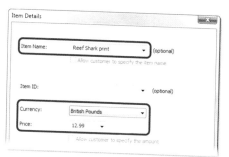

- **Item ID:** If you have a specific product code reference, enter it here. We left ours blank.

- **Currency:** Choose the currency required from the drop-down list.

- **Price:** Type the price of the item.

- Click **Next**.

5 The **Item Description** can be used to add extra details about the sale item. As we will have three different sizes of print for sale, we've listed the price of each size in the description.

We already have an image, so we don't need to add another.

Click **Next**.

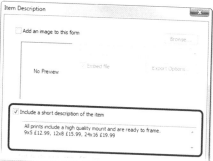

6 In the **Item Options** dialog click **Add Multiple Option...**

7 In the **Multiple Option** dialog:

- In the **Name** box, type 'Size'.

- In the **Prompt** box, type 'Size:'.

- Select **Option changes price**.

- Select the **Combo Box** option.

- Click **Add Option...**

For information on the other options in the dialog, see online Help.

8   In the **Option** dialog:

- In the **Name** box, type '9x5'.

- In the **Value** box, type '9x5 inches'.

- In the **Price** drop-down list, select 12.99.

- Click the **Selected** check box— this sets the item as the default option when the page opens.

- Click **Add Another**.

9   Repeat step 8 to create a '12x8' option, but this time:

- In the **Price** field, type '15.99'.

- Do not select the **Selected** check box—you can only set one default!

- Click **Add Another**.

10 Repeat step 9 to create a '24x16' option at '19.99' and then click **OK**.

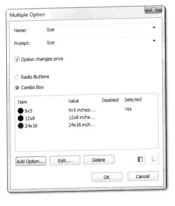

Your **Multiple Options** dialog should now list the three options you specified, as illustrated left.

Click **OK**.

11 The **Item Options** dialog displays again, allowing you to add further options. We don't want to do this so click **Next**.

12 In the **Item Details** dialog:

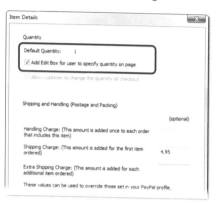

- Select the **Add Edit Box** option to let the customer define the quantity to be ordered.

- In the **Shipping and Handling** section, type the additional charges associated with the order item (if any). If these are left blank, the default profile set in PayPal will be used.

- Click **Next**.

13 In the **Extra Customer Information** dialog, select **Customer prompted for address** in the drop-down list and click **Next**.

14 In the **Payment Pages** dialog, leave the default settings and click **Next**.

15 In the **Form Layout** dialog, because we have more than one pricing option, clear the **Show price on form** option and click **Finish**.

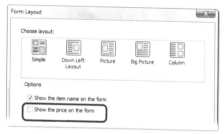

16 Click and drag on your page to insert the e-commerce form on your page, between the two column guidelines next to the image.

If necessary, you can move and adjust the individual form objects, and edit their appearance, as you would any other WebPlus object. We adjusted the position of the PayPal button.

We're now going to insert another e-commerce object into the space created—a **View Cart** button.

To insert a View Cart button

1 On the Web Objects toolbar, click the  **Insert an E-Commerce object** button.

2 In the **Add PayPal Object** dialog:

• Select the email address you used previously.

• Select the **View Shopping Cart Link** option.

• Click **Next**.

3 In the **Button Image** dialog:

• Select the **Use a standard image** option.

• Select the image you want to use.

• Click **Finish**.

4 Click to insert your button at default size, then drag it into position on your form.

5 Preview your page in your web browser. Check that you can:

• Select a **Size** from the drop-down list.

• Edit the product **Quantity**.

• Add items to your shopping cart.

• View your shopping cart.

If you're happy with the way your first product looks and functions, you can use it as a template for your other objects by simply copying and editing the form.

We'll do this next...

To copy and edit the form

1 Select the second empty picture frame on the page and click the 🗞 **Replace Picture** button.

2 Browse to locate the second image you want to sell on your website— we selected the **waves.jpg** file—and click **Open**.

The picture is added to the frame and scaled to maximum-fit as before.

Now we need to copy the e-commerce form and edit it to match this new item.

3 Click and drag to select the HTML print title frame and the form object.

4 Hold the **Ctrl** key and drag down to create a copy of the objects. Position these next to the second image.

5 Click inside the new HTML title frame and change the text to 'Ocean Waves print'.

💡 In our sample store, we only need to change the name of each item as all other options (for example, print size and price) stay the same.

When you create your own e-commerce site, the extent of the changes required in these dialogs will depend on the type of items you are listing for sale.

If your items are very different, you may prefer to simply create each form from scratch, rather than copying and editing your first page as we have done here.

6   Right-click on an empty part of the form and select **Edit E-commerce Form...**

7   In the **Add PayPal Object** dialog, click **Next**.

8   In the **Button Image** dialog, click **Next**.

9   In the **Items Details** dialog, check the details displayed and replace any that do not apply to your new item.

(In our case, we only needed to type in the new name for the image 'Ocean Waves'.)

Click **Next**.

10 In the **Item Description** dialog, replace any of the options that have changed for this new item. If the same options apply, as in our case, simply click **Next** to proceed.

11 Click **Next** (unless you want to add another option for this item).

12 In the **Item Details** dialog, edit the shipping and handling charges if required. If no changes are required, click **Next**.

13 In the **Extra Customer Information** dialog, click **Next**.

14 In the **Payment Pages** dialog, click **Next**.

15 In the **Form Layout** dialog, ensure that the **Reformat Form** option is cleared and click **Finish**.

The form is updated with the new details.

16 Preview the page in your browser.

Starting with empty picture frames for your images makes it very easy to create image thumbnails that all have the same dimensions, without changing the aspect ratio of the pictures they contain. For more information about using empty picture frames, see the *Pictures* tutorial.

Now that you have two objects in place, it's easy to add the rest of your product list.

17 Simply repeat the previous steps to insert a new page for each image thumbnail, replacing the image and editing the e-commerce form as required.

18 When you've added all of your pages, preview and test your e-commerce site in your web browser.

Your finished page should look something like ours.

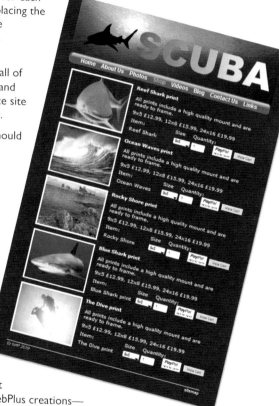

Congratulations, you've created your first e-commerce website! We hope you've enjoyed the exercise and wish you every success in your e-commerce ventures.

If you also worked through the other tutorials, you should by now be feeling very comfortable with WebPlus tools and well-equipped to start working on your own WebPlus creations— whether their purpose is personal or for profit!

 Search Engine Optimization

To learn about how you can attract visitors to your site (so that they can start purchasing those products!), see the *Search Engines* tutorial, available in PDF format from the Learning Zone.

iFrames

In this tutorial, we introduce inline frames or, more specifically, iFrames. We'll create a basic photo gallery by creating a page that uses iFrame technology.

In this project, you'll learn how to:

- Insert an iFrame onto a page.
- Create and link content that will appear within the iFrame.
- Clone pages.

IFrames

An inline frame, or iFrame, is a frame placed on your page and website. The content displayed within an iFrame can come from a separate page, document, or even an entire website! Because an iFrame works independently from the page that displays it, the iFrame can even have its own navigation elements—any link clicked inside the frame only changes the frame and not the page. This behaviour makes iFrames extremely useful for displaying large amounts of information in a small space, and if used well, are an effective tool.

Image page preview

Collection page

As site visitors click through the thumbnails on the left, the iFrame on the right updates with the corresponding full-size image and text.

iFrame pages

To demonstrate iFrames, we have created an example photography website for you to work on. The project file, **iframes.wpp**, and its images can be found in the **Workspace** folder.

To open the project file

1   On the Standard toolbar, click 📂 **Open**.

2   Navigate to the **Workspace** folder and click to select the **iframes.wpp** project file. In a typical installation, this folder is found in:

   C:\Program Files\Serif\WebPlus\X4\Tutorials

3   Click **Yes** in the dialog to open as a new, untitled site.

4   Click **File > Save As...** and save your new file under a new name.

5   On the **Site** tab, double-click on the **Collection** page entry.

   The page displays in the workspace.

Currently, the **Collection** page contains a set of small thumbnails but no additional content. We're going to add an inline frame so that our site visitors can view a larger version of the images and read the additional information.

The content of the iFrame will be dynamically changed, depending on which thumbnail is clicked. Sound complicated? Don't worry, it really isn't. Let's get started.

> 💡 To create the thumbnails, we placed six empty frames on the page and sized them using the **Transform** tab. The frames were aligned using the **Align** tab, before using the picture frame controls to replace and position our images. For more information, see the *Pictures* tutorial.

To insert an iFrame

1   On the Web Objects toolbar, click the ▢ **Framed Document Tool** and then click and drag to create a large frame on the right of your **Collection** page.

2   In the **Framed Document** dialog, click **OK** to accept the default settings—we'll come back to this later when we have created the content.

3   On the **Transform** tab, click the ⚲ **Lock Aspect Ratio** button to allow unconstrained resizing (it will change to ⚲). Change the Width to 405 pixels and the Height to 320 pixels.

4   If necessary, drag the iFrame into position on the page.

    That's all for now. The next step is to create a content page.

To create iFrame content pages

1   On the **Site** tab, click ▣ **Add** to add a new page.

2   In the **New Page Properties** dialog:

    • On the **Appearance** tab, in the **Placement** section, select Collection from the drop-down list.

    • Change the Width to 380 pixels.

- Click the **Navigation** tab.

- Change the **Page name** to **droplet**.

- Change the **File name** to **droplet.html**

- Clear **Include in Navigation**.

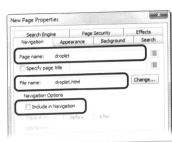

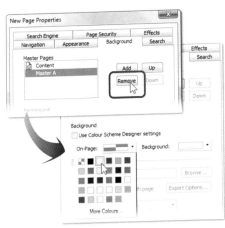

- Click the **Background** tab.

- Remove **Master A.**

- Clear **Use Colour Scheme Designer Settings** and change on-page colour to white.

- Click **OK**.

3 Working on the new page, on the Standard Objects toolbar, in the Picture flyout, click ⊠ **Empty Picture Frame**.

4 Place the frame in the top centre of the page, with the top edge of the frame aligned to the top of the page.

5 On the **Transform** tab, set the Width to **350** pixels and the Height to **250** pixels.

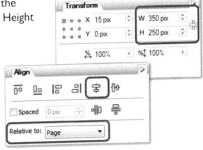

6 With the frame still selected, on the **Align** tab:

- Ensure that **Relative to: Page** is selected.

- Click ⊕ **Centre Horizontally**.

7 Finally, click the  **Replace Picture** button on the frame control bar.

8 Navigate to the **Workspace** folder and select droplet.png. Click **Open**.

9 If necessary, adjust the picture in the frame using the tools on the frame control bar.

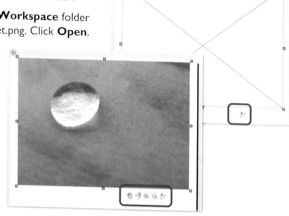

Next we'll pace an HTML text frame for the picture information.

10 On the Standard Objects toolbar, click the  **HTML Text Frame Tool**.

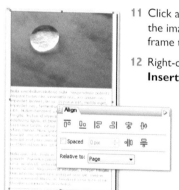

11 Click and drag to place the HTML frame below the image. On the **Transform** tab, resize the frame to 330 pixels wide x 350 pixels high.

12 Right-click inside the HTML frame and click **Insert > Placeholder text**.

13 Finally, select both objects and, on the **Align** tab, click **Centre Horizontally, Relative to: Page**.

The first content page is complete. Luckily, we can quickly create the other five content pages without having to repeat all of the steps.

To clone pages

1 In the **Site** tab, right-click the page entry for the **droplet** page and select **Clone Page**.

2 Right-click the new page and select **Page Properties...** In the **Navigation** tab, change the **Page name** to **poppy head** and the **File name** to **poppy head.html**.

3 Click the 🖼 **Replace Picture** button on the frame control bar and browse to the **poppy head.png** Workspace file.

Notice that the picture is sized fit the existing space perfectly. This is the main advantage for working with picture frames when creating multiple pages from the same template.

4 Repeat steps 1 to 3 for each of the remaining thumbnail images—**waves.jpg**, **clouds.png**, **MG.jpg** and **shore.jpg**.

Now that we have the iFrame content complete, your site tab should resemble the one illustrated. The next step is to link the iFrame to its content.

To link the iFrame to its content

1 On the **Site** tab, double-click the **Collection** page entry.

2 Right-click the iFrame and click **Edit Framed Document...**

3 In the **Framed Document** dialog:

- Select the **Site Page** option.

- In the **Page name** drop-down list, select **droplet**.

- If you want users to be able to bookmark to the image frame, select the **Export as absolute URL** check box; otherwise leave this unchecked.

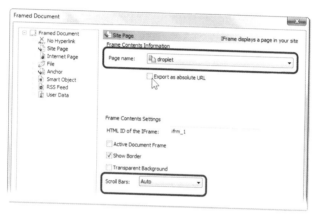

- Leave **Scroll Bars** set to **Auto**.

- Click **OK**.

We've just linked our iFrame to the page showing the full-size version of our first thumbnail. Now, when visitors first view the **Collection** page, this image will be displayed in the frame.

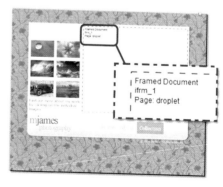

Our final task is to link the image thumbnails to the content pages, so that when visitors click on the thumbnail, the full-size image will display in the iFrame.

To link the thumbnails

1 On the **Collection** page, right-click the matching image thumbnail for the **droplet** page and select **Hyperlink**.

2 In the **Hyperlinks** dialog:

   • Select **Site Page**.

   • In the **Page name** drop-down list, select **droplet**.

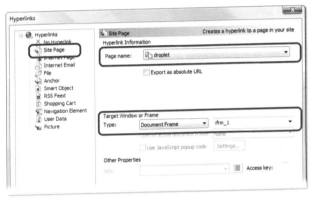

   • In the **Type** drop-down list, select **Document Frame**, and check that **ifrm_1** is selected in the corresponding list.

   • Click **OK**.

   The image will now display in the frame when the thumbnail is clicked.

   Note: You won't be able to see the effect of this step when previewing your site until you've linked the other thumbnails!

3 Repeat steps 1 and 2 for each of the remaining thumbnails.

4 Finally, click ⌨▾ **Preview Site in {browser of choice}**.

5 Click on each of the thumbnails to ensure that each page loads correctly inside the iFrame.

⚠ **When not to use iFrames**

As a general rule of thumb, you should not use iFrames to link to e-commerce content as it can interfere with security certificates.

That's it! You have successfully created a site that uses iFrames! By now, you should have the knowledge to use iFrames within your own site. The possibilities are virtually endless. Why not try using them in conjunction with some of the **Serif Web Resources** smart objects?

Have fun!

Theme Layouts

Introduction

WebPlus includes a selection of theme layouts that you can use as starting points for your own sites.

Available from the Startup Wizard, the theme layouts offer a range of layout styles. Each layout comes complete with picture and text placeholders, and offers a choice of purpose-built site pages.

To open a theme layout:

1 In the **Startup Wizard**, click **Create > Use Design Template**.

2 In the **Create New Site From Template** dialog:

- Browse the **Theme Layouts** category and select the layout you want to use.

- Choose a colour scheme from the drop-down list.

  You can choose from three schemes specially designed to complement the theme layout, or you can apply any of the colour schemes included with WebPlus.

- In the **Pages** pane, choose the site pages to include in the layout by selecting their check boxes.

- Click **Open**.

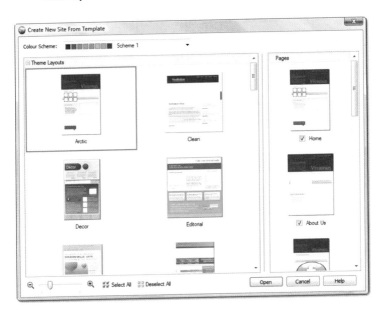

The following pages provide previews of the **Theme Layout** templates included on the **WebPlus X4 Program CD**.

Arctic

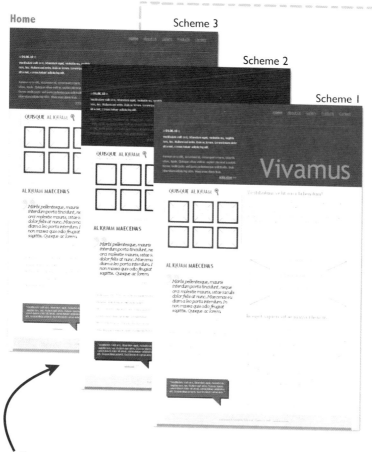

💡 Each layout offers three colour scheme options specific to that template, but you can also experiment with the other predefined colour schemes, or make your own custom scheme.

At any time during the design process, you can use the **Colour Scheme Designer** to choose a new colour scheme for your site.

For more on colour schemes and the **Colour Scheme Designer**, see online Help and the *Colour Schemes* tutorial.

About Us

Gallery

Products

Contact

Adding new pages

1 Expand the **Site** tab's ⊞ ▾ **Add new page** drop-down list.

2 Click **New Blank Page** to insert a blank page (based on your layout).

- or -

Click **New Template Page...** to open the **Add New Page From Template** dialog, then choose from a range of purpose-built site pages.

Pages not included in navigation:

- Article 01
- Article 02
- Links
- Terms & conditions

Clean

Home

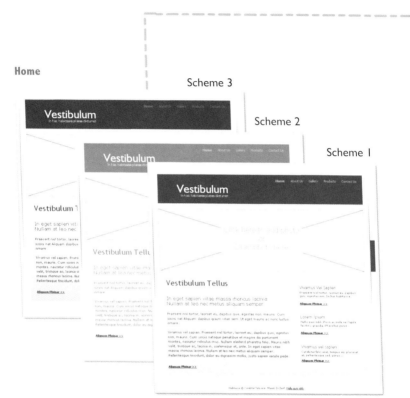

Scheme 3

Scheme 2

Scheme 1

About Us

Gallery

Products

Contact

Pages not included in navigation:

- Article 01
- Article 02
- Links
- Terms & conditions

Decor

Home

Scheme 3

Scheme 2

Scheme 1

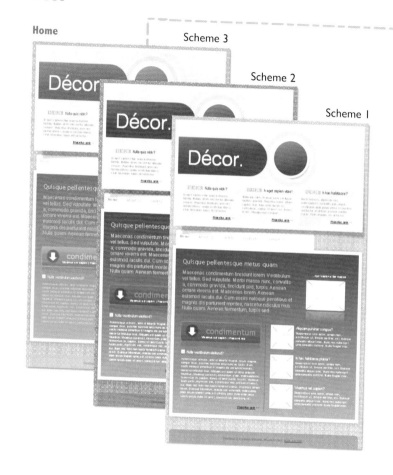

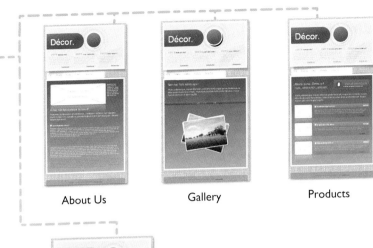

About Us

Gallery

Products

Contact

Pages not included in navigation:

- Article 01
- Article 02
- Links
- Terms & conditions

Editorial

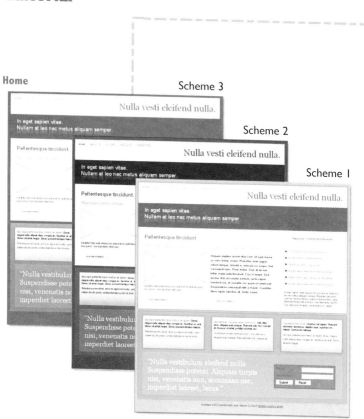

Home

Scheme 3

Scheme 2

Scheme 1

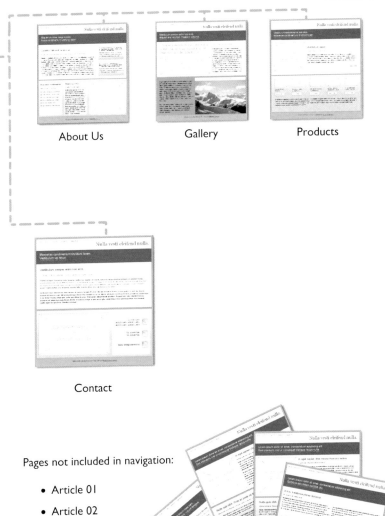

About Us

Gallery

Products

Contact

Pages not included in navigation:

- Article 01
- Article 02
- Links
- Terms & conditions

Mode

Home

About Us

Gallery

Products

Contact

Pages not included in navigation:

- Article 01
- Article 02
- Links
- Terms & conditions

Natural

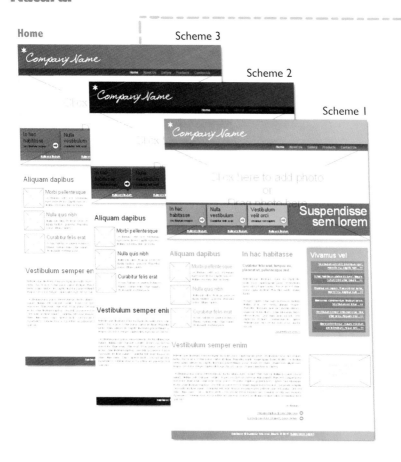

Home

Scheme 3

Scheme 2

Scheme 1

About Us

Gallery

Products

Contact

Pages not included in navigation:

- Article 01
- Article 02
- Links
- Terms & conditions

Solid

Home

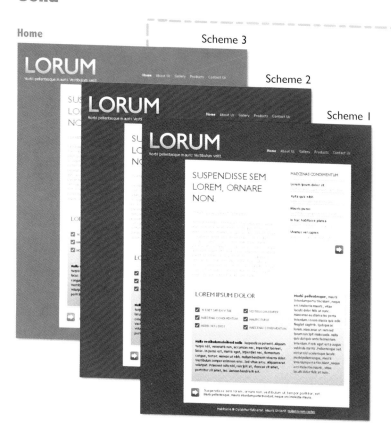

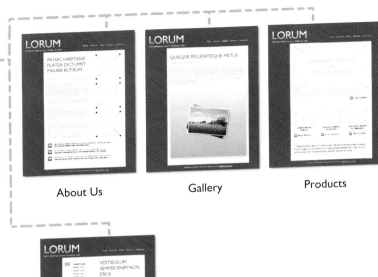

About Us

Gallery

Products

Contact

Pages not included in navigation:

- Article 01
- Article 02
- Links
- Terms & conditions

Spiro

Home

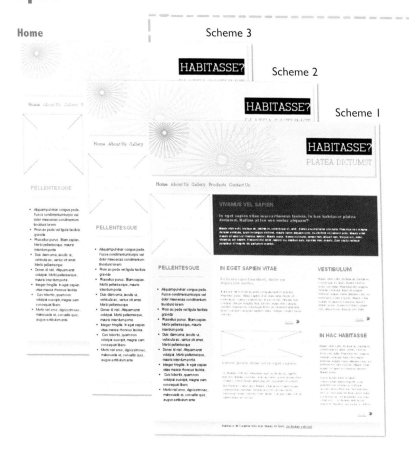

Scheme 3

Scheme 2

Scheme 1

About Us   Gallery   Products

Contact

Pages not included in navigation:

- Article 01
- Article 02
- Links
- Terms & conditions

Tabs

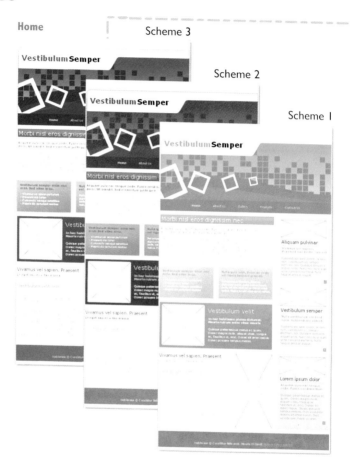

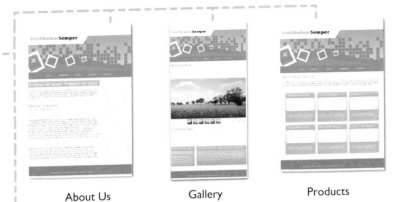

About Us   Gallery   Products

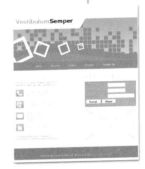

Contact

Pages not included in navigation:

- Article 01
- Article 02
- Links
- Terms & conditions

Tickle

Home

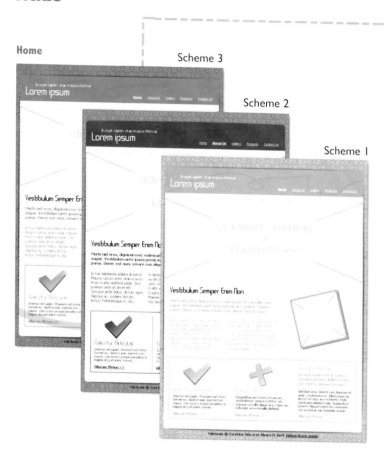

Scheme 3

Scheme 2

Scheme 1

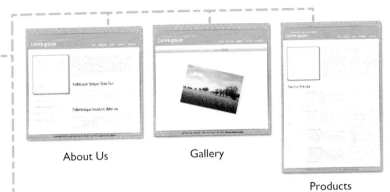

About Us

Gallery

Products

Contact

Pages not included in navigation:

- Article 01
- Article 02
- Links
- Terms & conditions

Navigation Bars

Introduction

WebPlus includes a selection of customizable JavaScript and Flash™ navigation bars that you can add to your own sites.

The following navigation bar types are provided:

- Basic (JavaScript)
- Designer (JavaScript)
- Miscellaneous (JavaScript)
- Basic (Flash)
- Designer (Flash)

For more information on navigation bars, see the *Navigation Bars* tutorial, and *Adding navigation bars* in online Help.

To insert a navigation bar:

1   On the Web Objects toolbar, click
    Insert Navigation Bar.

    - or -

    Open the **QuickBuilder Bar** and drag
    the **Navigation Bar** icon onto your
    page.

2   In the **Navigation Bar Settings** dialog:

    • Select a category from the **Type** drop-down list.

    • Browse to and select the navigation bar you want to use, and then
      click **Select**.

    • Choose your other settings from the **Navigation Type**, **Options**,
      and **Style** tabs.

    • Click **OK**.

The following pages provide previews of the navigation bars included on
the **WebPlus X4 Program CD**.

Basic (JavaScript)

Basic Menu Style 1-1

Home   Products   Gallery   About Us

History

Basic Menu Style 2-1

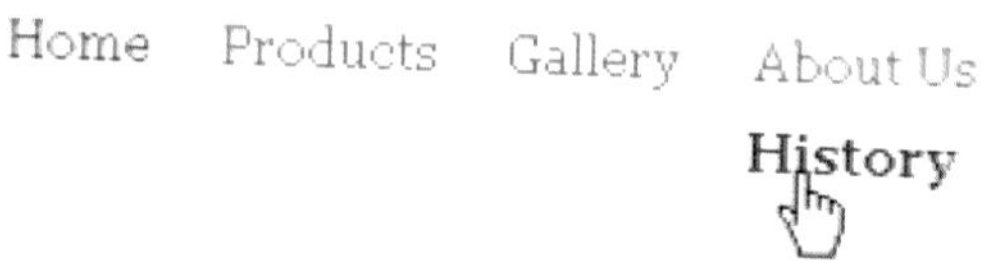

Home   Products   Gallery   About Us

History

Basic Menu Style 3-1

Home   Products   Gallery   About Us

History

Basic Menu Style 4-1

Home   Products   Gallery   About Us

History

Basic Menu Style 5-1

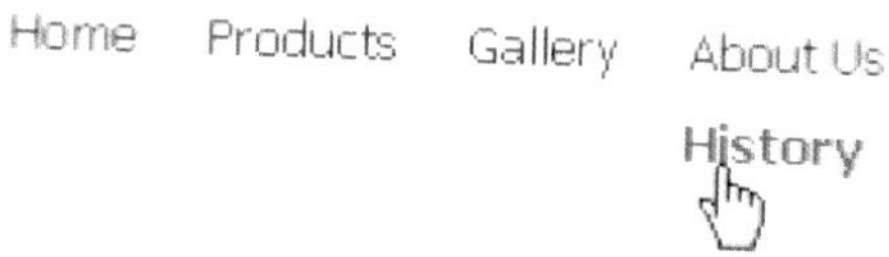

Home   Products   Gallery   About Us

History

Basic Menu Style 6-1

Home   Products   Gallery   About Us
                                History

Basic Menu Style 7-1

Home   Products   Gallery   About Us
                                History

Basic Menu Style 8-1

Home   Products   Gallery   About Us
                                History

Basic Menu Style 9-1

Home | Products | Gallery | About Us

Basic Menu Style 10-1

Home * Products * Gallery * About Us

Home - Products - Gallery - About Us

History

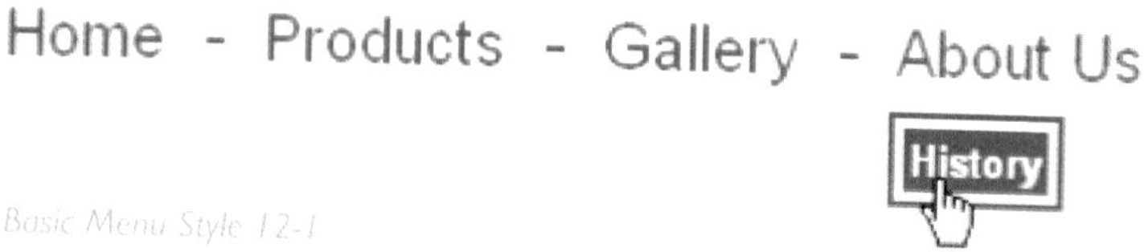

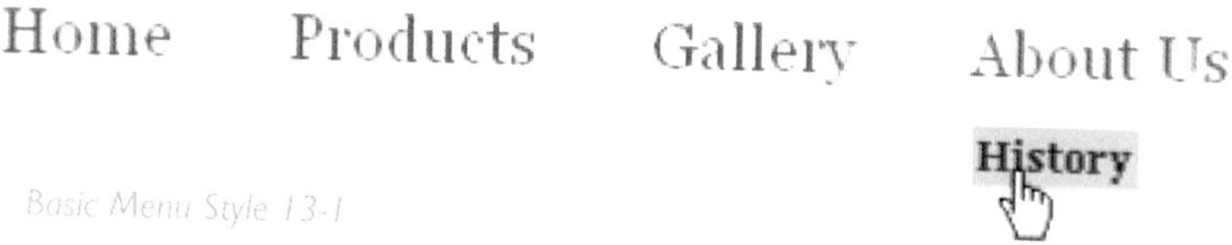

Home   Products   Gallery   About Us

History

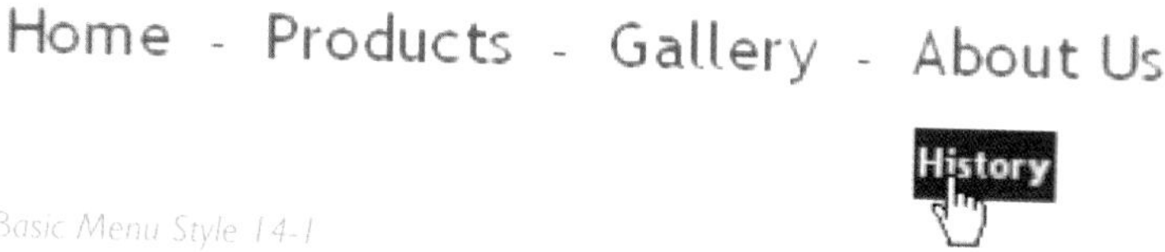

Home - Products - Gallery - About Us

History

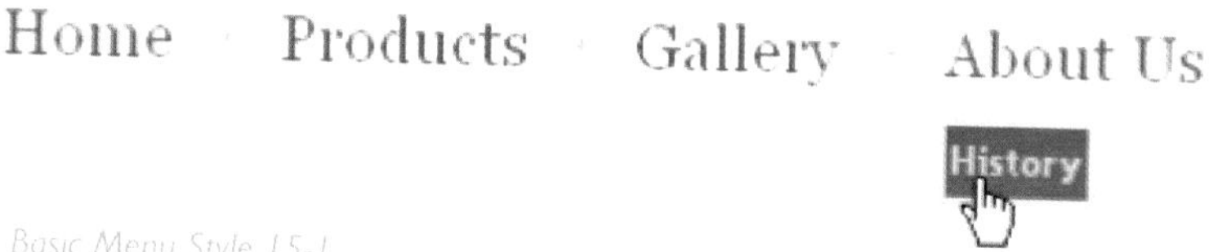

Home   Products   Gallery   About Us

History

Home | Products | Gallery | About Us

History

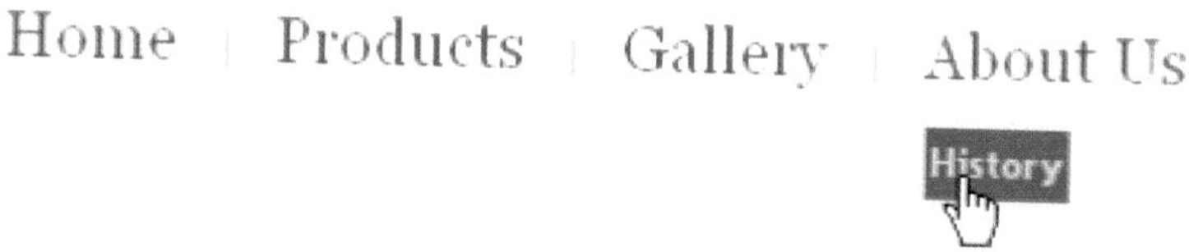

Basic Menu Style 16-1

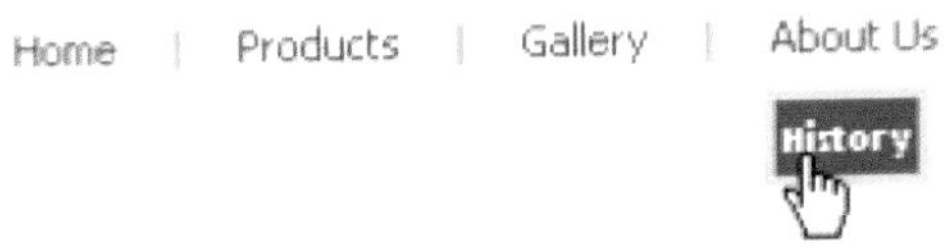

Home | Products | Gallery | About Us

History

Basic Menu Style 17-1

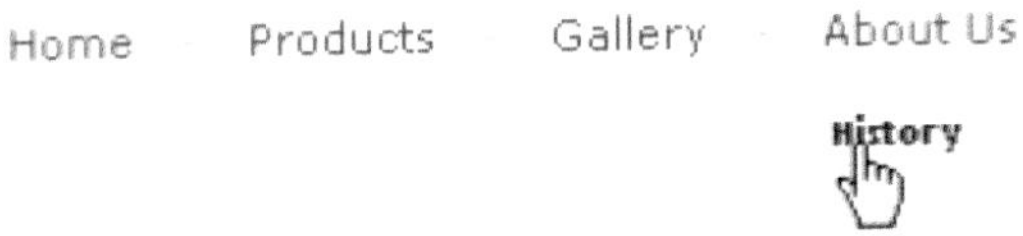

Home   Products   Gallery   About Us

History

Basic Menu Style 18-1

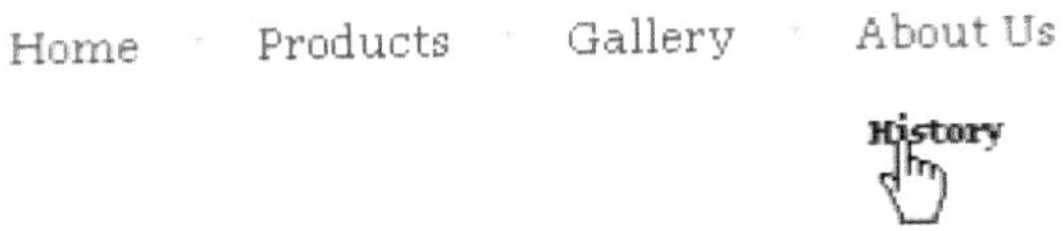

Home   Products   Gallery   About Us

History

Basic Menu Vertical Style 1-1

Home
Products
Gallery
About Us **History**

Basic Menu Vertical Style 2-1

Home
Products
Gallery
About Us **History**

Basic Menu Vertical Style 3-1

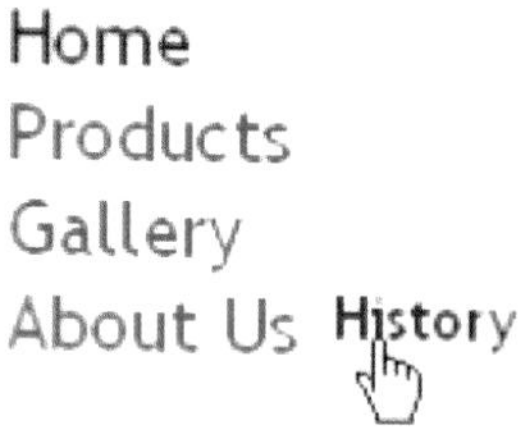

Basic Menu Vertical Style 4-1

Home
Products
Gallery
About Us **History**

Home
Products
Gallery
About Us **History**

Basic Menu Vertical Style 5-1

Basic Menu Vertical Style 6-1

Home
Products
Gallery
About Us **History**

Home
Products
Gallery
About Us **History**

Basic Menu Vertical Style 7-1

Basic Menu Vertical Style 8-1

Home
Products
Gallery
About Us History

Home
Products
Gallery
About Us **History**

Designer (JavaScript)

Designer Menu Style 1-1

Designer Menu Style 2-1

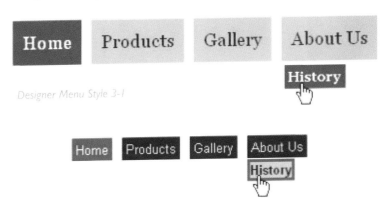

Designer Menu Style 3-1

Designer Menu Style 4-1

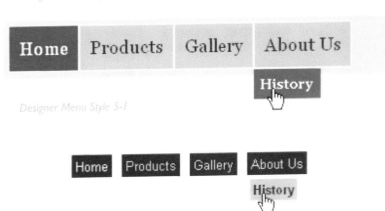

Designer Menu Style 5-1

Designer Menu Style 6-1

Designer Menu Style 7-1

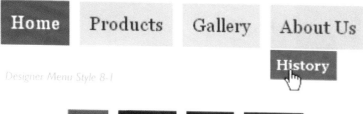

Designer Menu Style 8-1

Designer Menu Style 9-1

Designer Menu Style 10-1

Designer Menu Style 11-1

Designer Menu Style 12-1

Designer Menu Style 13-1

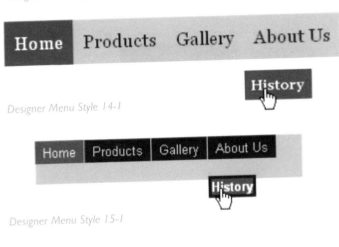

Designer Menu Style 14-1

Designer Menu Style 15-1

Designer Menu Style 16-1

Designer Menu Style 17-1

Designer Menu Vertical Style 1-1

Designer Menu Vertical Style 2-1

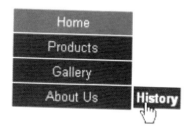

Basic Menu Vertical Style 3-1

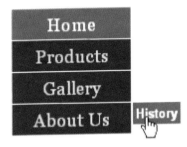

Basic Menu Vertical Style 4-1

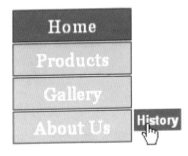

Basic Menu Vertical Style 5-1

Designer Menu Vertical Style 6-1

Designer Menu Vertical Style 7-1

Gel-1

Plain-1

Rounded-1

Miscellaneous (JavaScript)

Default-1

Site Map Style 1-1

Home
Products
Gallery
About Us
History

Site Map Style 2-1

Home
Products
Gallery
About Us
History

Buttons Style 1-1

Home

Products

Gallery

About Us   ▼

History

Basic Menu Vertical Style 3-1

Home
Products
Gallery
About Us

Basic Menu Vertical Style 5-1

Basic (Flash)

Arrow Pointer Style 1-1

Home   Products   Gallery   ▼ About Us

History

Arrow Pointer Style 2-1

▲ Home   ▲ Products   ▲ Gallery   ▶ About Us
History

Arrow Pointer Style 3-1

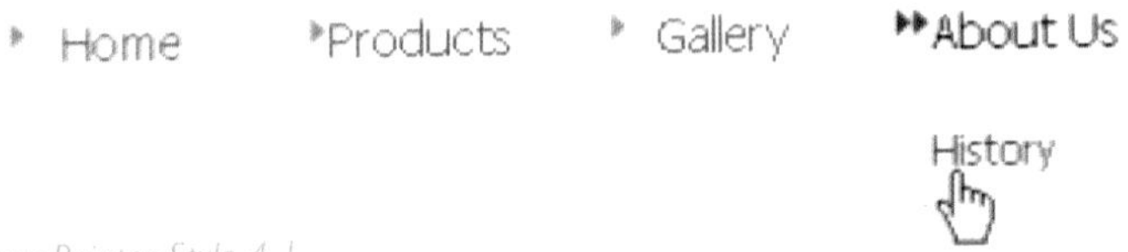

▶ Home   ▶Products   ▶ Gallery   ▶▶About Us

History

Arrow Pointer Style 4-1

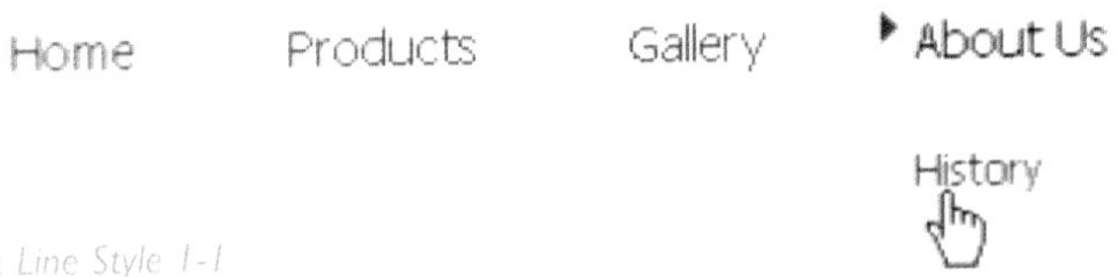

Home   Products   Gallery   ▶ About Us

History

Block Line Style 1-1

Home   Products   Gallery   About Us
_____   _____   _____   ▬▬▬▬▬
History

Block Line Style 2-1

| Home | Products | Gallery | ■ About Us |

History

Block Line Style 3-1

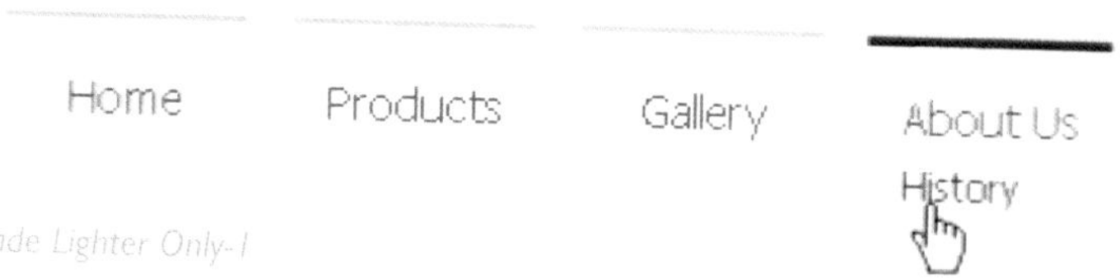

| Home | Products | Gallery | About Us |

History

Fade Lighter Only-1

| Home | Products | Gallery | About Us |

History

Fade Lighter with Dividers-1

| Home | Products | Gallery | About Us |

History

Fade Only-1

| Home | Products | Gallery | About Us |

History

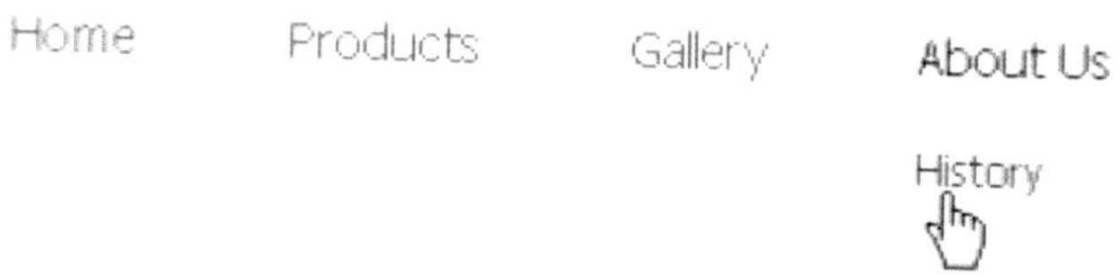

Fade with Dividers-1

| Home | Products | Gallery | About Us |

History

Fade with Underline-1

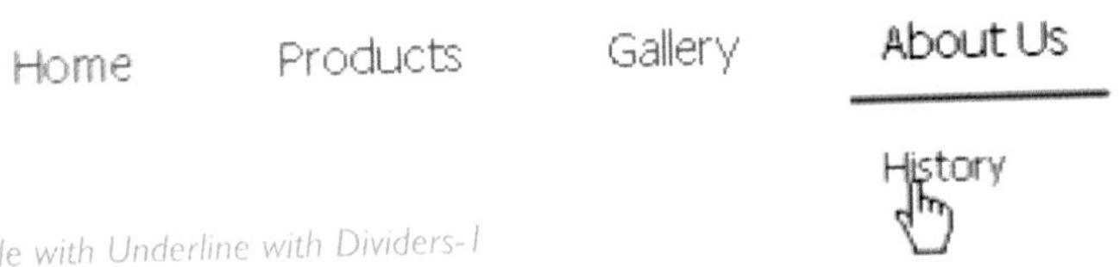

Home   Products   Gallery   **About Us**

History

Fade with Underline with Dividers-1

| Home | Products | Gallery | About Us |

History

Fade with Underline Jump-1

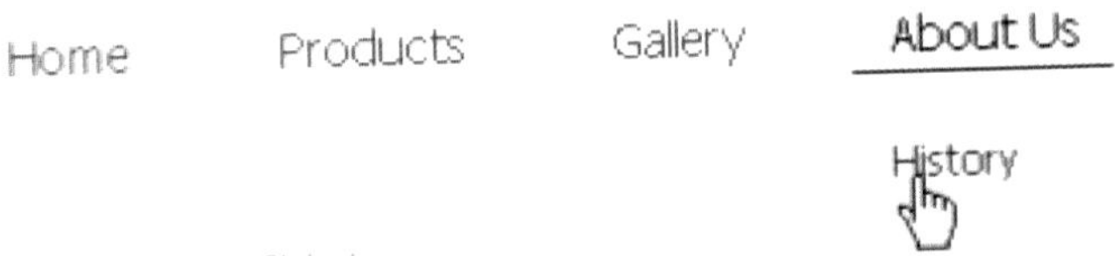

Home   Products   Gallery   About Us

History

Fade with Underline Slide-1

Home   Products   Gallery   About Us

History

Arrow Pointer Style 1 with Dropdown

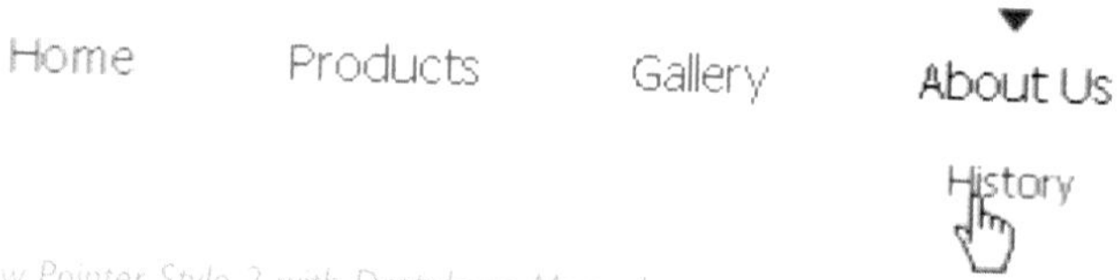

Home Products Gallery ▼ About Us

History

Arrow Pointer Style 2 with Dropdown Menu-1

▴ Home ▴ Products ▴ Gallery ▶ About Us

History

Arrow Pointer Style 3 with Dropdown Menu-1

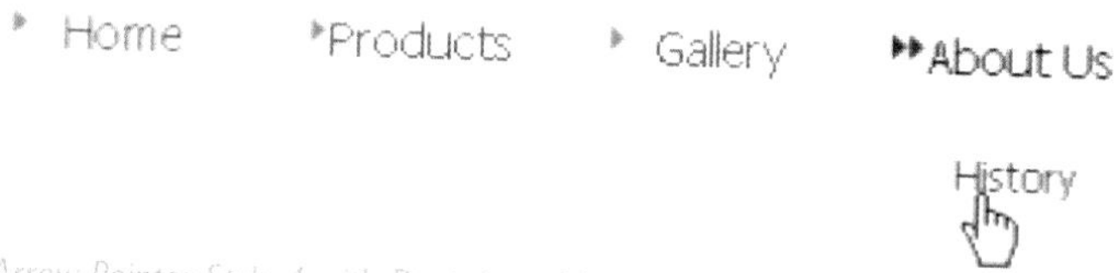

▶ Home ▶ Products ▶ Gallery ▶▶ About Us

History

Arrow Pointer Style 4 with Dropdown Menu-1

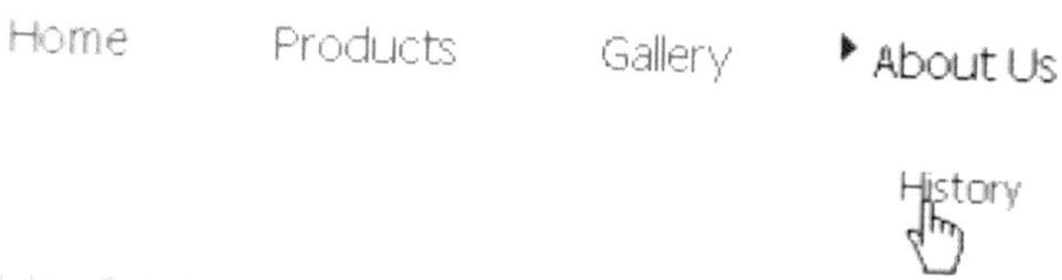

Home Products Gallery ▶ About Us

History

Block Line Style 1 with Dropdown Menu-1

Home Products Gallery About Us

History

Block Line Style 2 with Dropdown Menu-1

| Home | Products | Gallery | ▇ About Us |

History

Block Line Style 3 with Dropdown Menu-1

Home · Products · Gallery · **About Us**

History

Fade Lighter Only with Dropdown Menu-1

Home · Products · Gallery · About Us

History

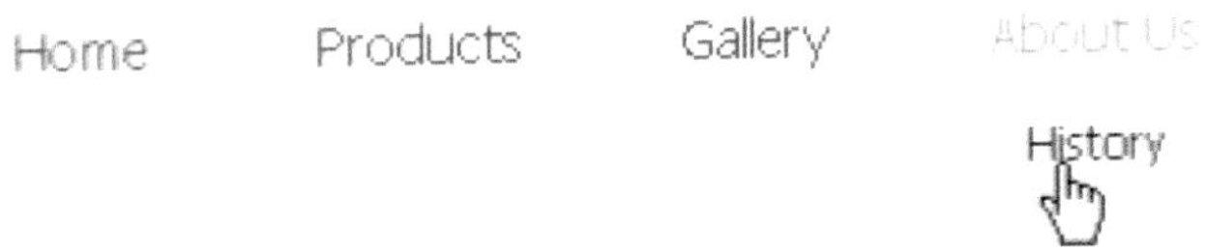

Fade Lighter with Dividers with Dropdown Menu-1

Home | Products | Gallery | About Us

History

Fade Only with Dropdown Menu-1

Home · Products · Gallery · About Us

History

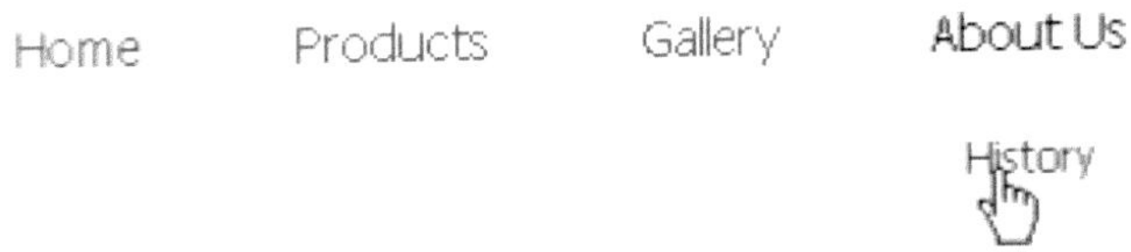

Fade with Dividers with Dropdown Menu-1

| Home | Products | Gallery | About Us |

History

Fade with Underline with Dropdown Menu-2

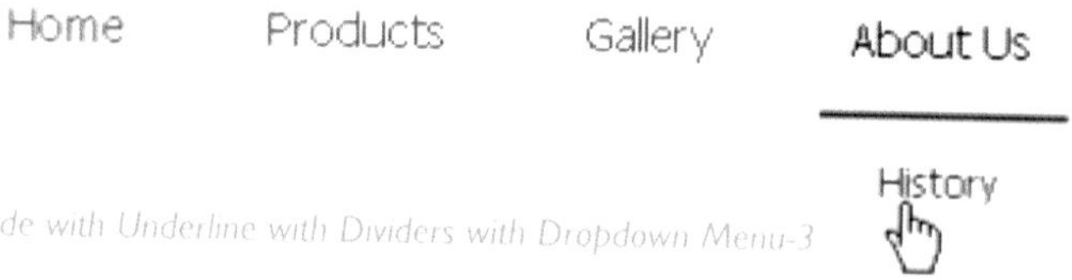

| Home | Products | Gallery | About Us |

History

Fade with Underline with Dividers with Dropdown Menu-3

| Home | Products | Gallery | About Us |

History

Fade with Underline Jump with Dropdown Menu-1

| Home | Products | Gallery | About Us |

History

Fade with Underline Slide with Dropdown Menu-1

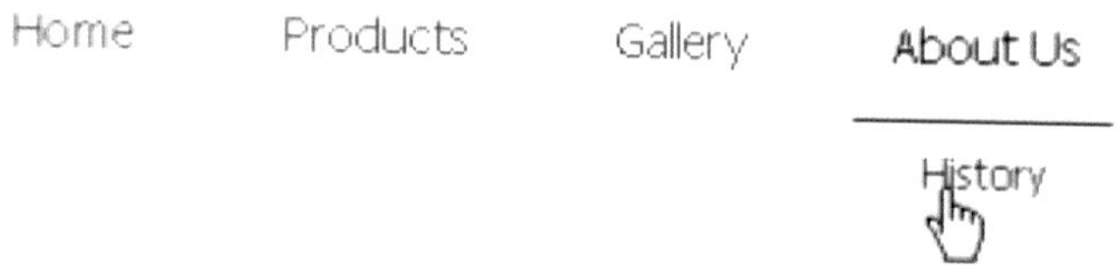

| Home | Products | Gallery | About Us |

History

Arrow Pointer Style 1 Vertical-1

Home

Products

Gallery

▼

About Us

History

Arrow Pointer Style 2 Vertical-1

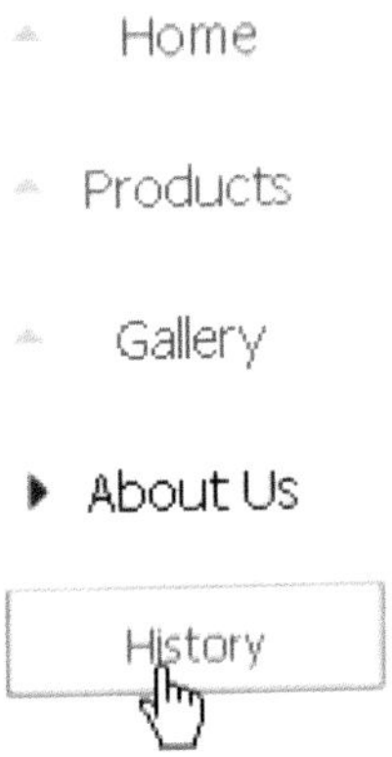

▲ Home

▲ Products

▲ Gallery

▶ About Us

History

Arrow Pointer Style 3 Vertical-1

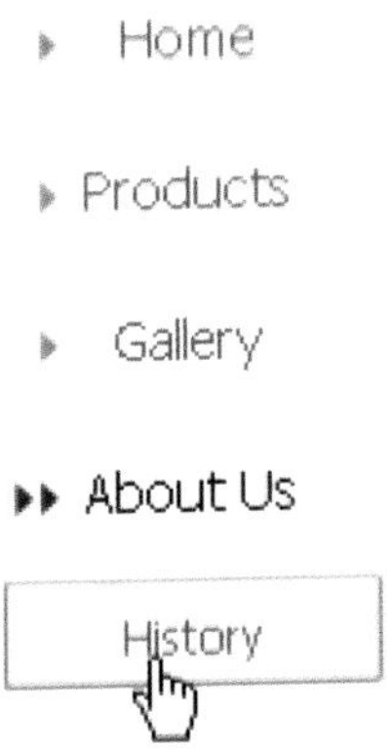

▸ Home

▸ Products

▸ Gallery

▸▸ About Us

History

Arrow Pointer Style 4 Vertical-1

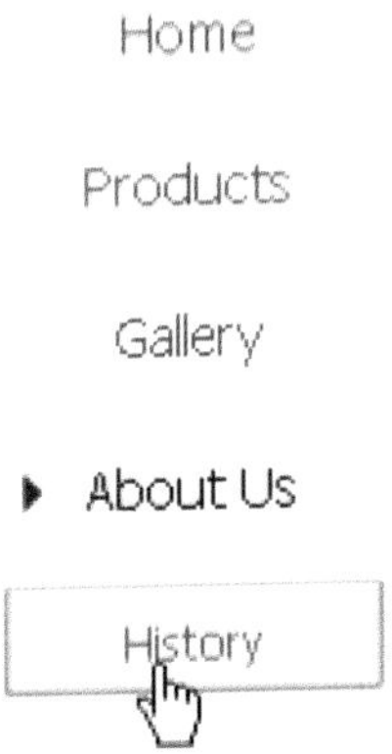

Home

Products

Gallery

▶ About Us

History

Block Line Style 1 Vertical-1

Home
_____
Products
_____
Gallery
_____
About Us

History

Block Line Style 2 Vertical-1

■ Home

■ Products

■ Gallery

■ About Us

History

Block Line Style 3 Vertical-1

_____
Home
_____
Products
_____
Gallery
_____
About Us

History

Fade Lighter Only Vertical-1

Home

Products

Gallery

About Us

History

Fade Lighter with Dividers Vertical-1   *Fade Only Vertical-1*

Home

Products

Gallery

About Us

History

Home

Products

Gallery

About Us

History

Fade with Dividers Vertical-1    *Fade with Underline Vertical-1*

Home

Products

Gallery

About Us

History

Home

Products

Gallery

About Us

History

Arrow Pointer Style 1 Vertical-1

Home
Products
Gallery
About Us
History

Arrow Pointer Style 2 Vertical-1

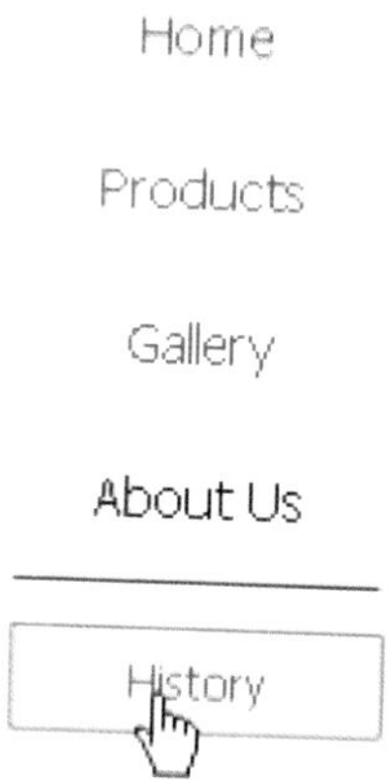

Home
Products
Gallery
About Us
History

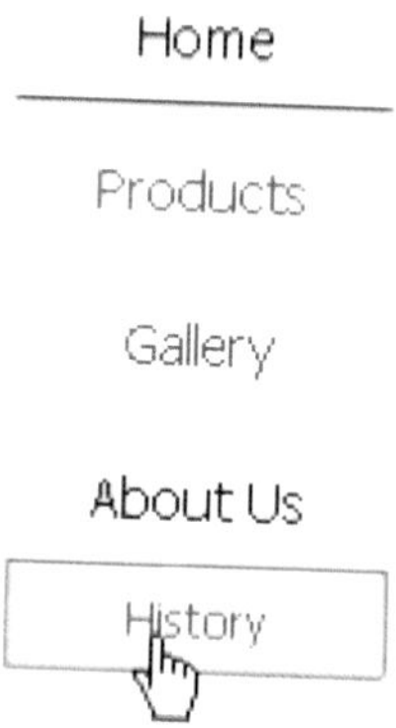

Designer (Flash)

Designer 1-1

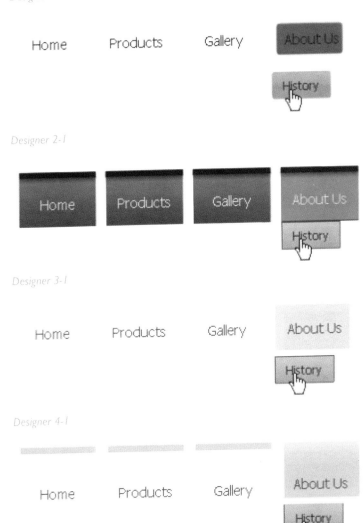

Designer 2-1

Designer 3-1

Designer 4-1

Designer 5-1

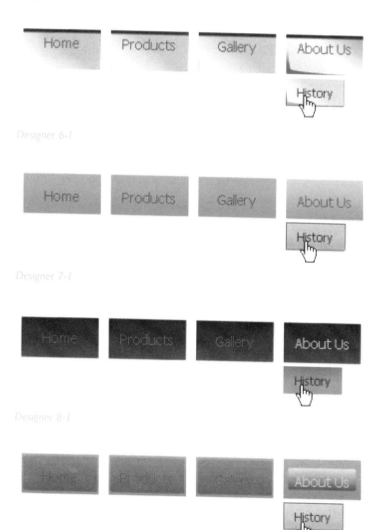

Designer 6-1

Designer 7-1

Designer 8-1

Designer 9-1

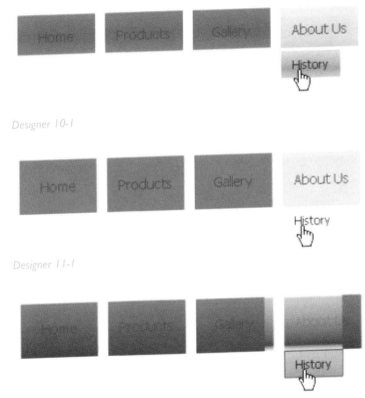

Designer 10-1

Designer 11-1

Designer 12-1

Designer 5 with Dropdown Menu-1

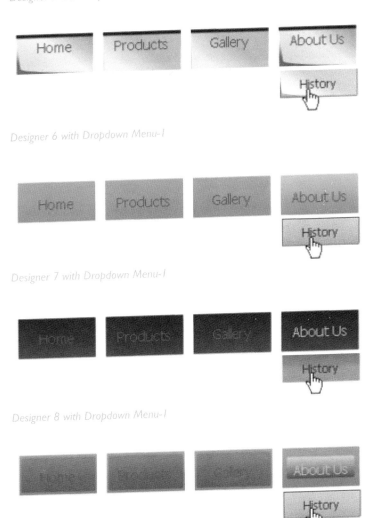

Designer 6 with Dropdown Menu-1

Designer 7 with Dropdown Menu-1

Designer 8 with Dropdown Menu-1

Designer 9 with Dropdown Menu-1

Designer 10 with Dropdown Menu-1

Designer 11 with Dropdown Menu-1

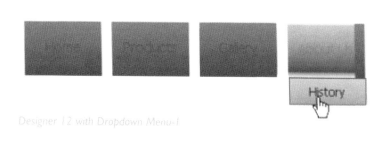

Designer 12 with Dropdown Menu-1

Designer 1 Vertical-1

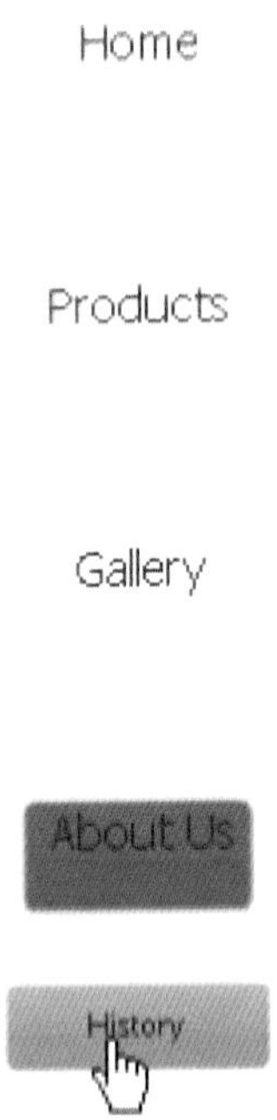
Home
Products
Gallery
About Us
History

Designer 2 Vertical-1

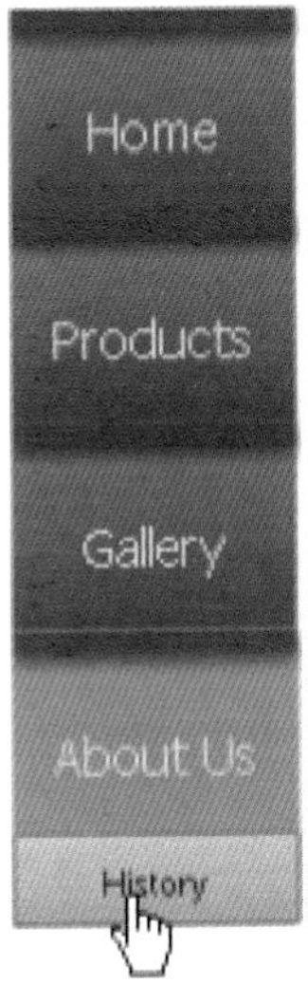
Home
Products
Gallery
About Us
History

Designer 3 Vertical-1

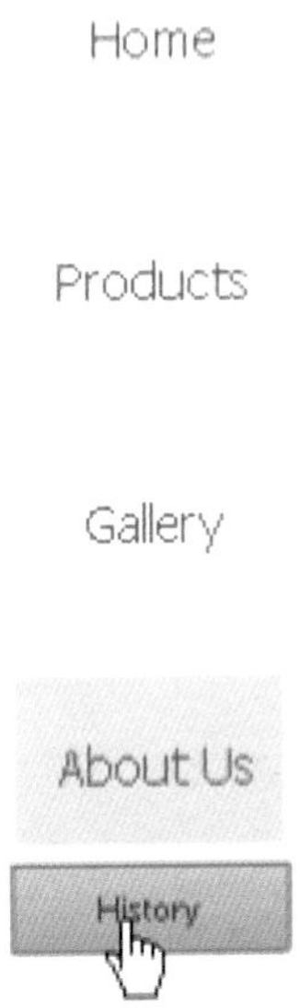
Home
Products
Gallery
About Us
History

Designer 4 Vertical-1

Home

Products

Gallery

About Us

History

Designer 5 Vertical-1

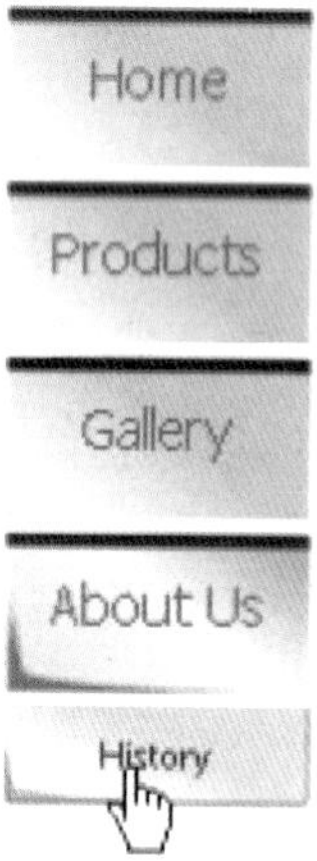

Home

Products

Gallery

About Us

History

Designer 6 Vertical-1

Home

Products

Gallery

About Us

History

Designer 7 Vertical-1

Designer 8 Vertical-1

Designer 9 Vertical-1

Designer 10 Vertical-1

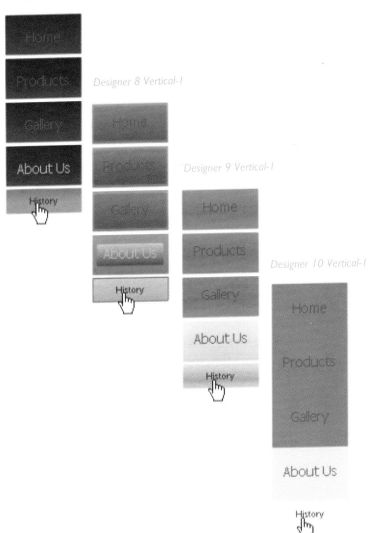

Website &
Email Templates

Introduction

Website templates

WebPlus X4 provides a selection of website design templates, which you can use as starting points for your own sites.

The following categories are included:

- Business
- E-Commerce
- Entertainment
- Interest
- Personal

Email templates

Also included are a collection of email templates, grouped into two categories: Business and Home.

These templates are fully customizable—whatever the occasion, it has never been easier to share your news!

You'll find a wide range of additional design templates in Serif **Premium Template Packs 1 & 2** for WebPlus.

For details, see the Serif website.

To open a template:

1 In the **Startup Wizard**, click **Create > Use Design Template**.

2 In the **Create New Site From Template** dialog:

- Expand and browse the template categories and select the template you want to use.

- Choose a colour scheme from the drop-down list.

  You can choose from three schemes specially designed to complement the template, or you can apply any of the colour schemes included with WebPlus.

- In the **Pages** pane, choose the site pages to include in the layout by selecting their check boxes.

3 Click **Open**.

The following pages provide previews of the templates available on the **WebPlus X4 Program CD** and **Resource CD**.

Djs Vintage

About us

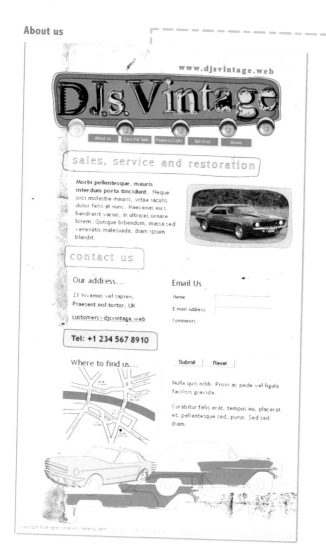

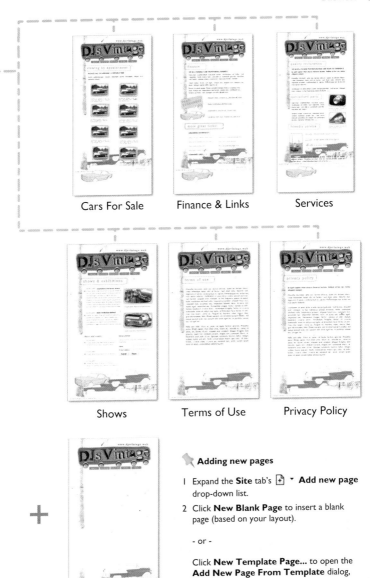

Cars For Sale

Finance & Links

Services

Shows

Terms of Use

Privacy Policy

Blank Page

Adding new pages

1 Expand the **Site** tab's ⊞ ▾ **Add new page** drop-down list.

2 Click **New Blank Page** to insert a blank page (based on your layout).

- or -

Click **New Template Page...** to open the **Add New Page From Template** dialog, then choose from a range of purpose-built site pages.

Ford Bennett

Home

FORD-BENNETT | Law Firm
Bringing justice to those who need it

- Home
- About
- Services
- Industry Updates
- Contacts

finance • litigation • commercial • corporate • real estate

Welcome

Finance

Volutpat. Integer fringilla. Duis lobortis, quam non volutpat suscipit, magna a em consequat libero, ac hendrerit urna ante id mi. Quisque commodo facilisis tellus.

Litigation

Integer sodales lorem a sed nisl Morbi consectetuer mauris quis odio. Ut dolor lorem, viverra vitae, viverra eu, euismod nec, enim. Lorem ipsum dolor sit amet, consectetuer adipiscing elit.

Commercial

Morbi nisl eros, dignissim nec, malesuada at, convallis quis, augue. Vestibulum ante ipsum primis in faucibus orci luctus et ultrices posuere cubilia Curae; Proin aliquam, leo ac luctus tempus, augue. Fusce in nisl vitae massa venenatis rhoncus. Praesent orci velit, lobortis eget, suscipit semper.

Corporate

Volutpat. Integer fringilla. Duis lobortis, quam non volutpat suscipit, magna a em consequat libero, ac hendrerit urna ante id mi. Quisque commodo facilisis tellus.

Real Estate

Integer sodales lorem a sed nisl Morbi consectetuer mauris quis odio. Ut dolor lorem, viverra vitae, viverra eu, euismod nec, enim. Lorem ipsum dolor sit amet, consectetuer adipiscing elit.

Integer sodales lorem a sed nisl Morbi consectetuer mauris quis odio. Ut dolor lorem, viverra vitae, viverra eu, euismod nec, enim. Lorem ipsum dolor sit amet, consectetuer adipiscing elit.

Finance

Volutpat. Integer fringilla. Duis lobortis, quam non volutpat suscipit, magna a em consequat libero, ac hendrerit urna ante id mi. Quisque commodo facilisis tellus.

Litigation

Integer sodales lorem a sed nisl Morbi consectetuer mauris quis odio. Ut dolor lorem, viverra vitae, viverra eu, euismod nec, enim. Lorem ipsum dolor sit amet, consectetuer adipiscing elit.

Commercial

Morbi nisl eros, dignissim nec, malesuada at, convallis quis, augue. Vestibulum ante ipsum primis in faucibus orci luctus et ultrices posuere cubilia Curae; Proin aliquam, leo ac luctus tempus, augue. Fusce in nisl vitae massa venenatis rhoncus. Praesent orci velit, lobortis eget, suscipit semper.

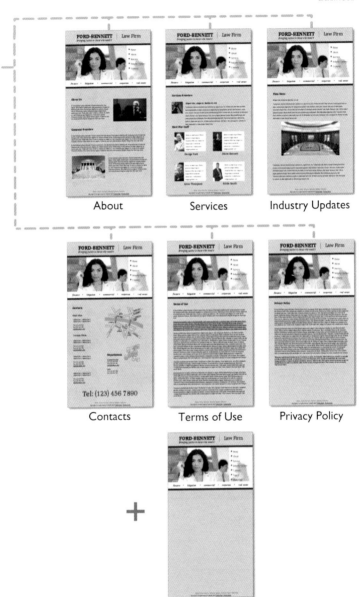

About

Services

Industry Updates

Contacts

Terms of Use

Privacy Policy

Tel: (123) 456 7890

+

Blank Page

Languages @ Home

Home

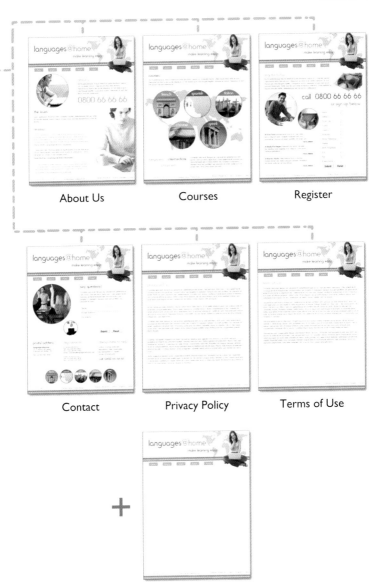

About Us

Courses

Register

Contact

Privacy Policy

Terms of Use

+

Blank Page

Medi247

Company Info

Welcome

Vivamus vel sapien. Praesent nisl tortor, laoreet eu, dapibus quis, egestas non, mauris. Cum sociis natoque penatibus et magnis dis parturient montes, nascetur ridiculus mus. Nullam eleifend pharetra felis. Mauris nibh velit, tristique ac, lacinia in, scelerisque et, ante.

Latest News

- 16.04.2009
In eget sapien vitae massa rhoncus lacinia. Nullam at leo nec metus aliquam semper. more>

- 11.03.2009
In eget sapien vitae massa rhoncus lacinia. more>

- 02.03.2009
Vivamus vel sapien. Praesent nisl tortor, laoreet eu, dapibus quis, egestas non, mauris. more>

- 24.03.2009
Morbi nisl eros, dignissim nec, malesuada et, convallis quis. more>

What We Offer

Morbi nisl eros, dignissim nec, malesuada et, convallis quis, augue. Vestibulum ante ipsum primis in faucibus orci luctus et ultrices posuere cubilia Curae; Proin aliquam, leo at luctus tempus.

- Vivamus vel sapien.
- Aliquam vel quam ut tellus.
- Aliquam dapibus ipsum.
- In eget sapien vitae massa.
- Nulla quis nibh.

Company Info   Patient Care   Services   Careers   Contact

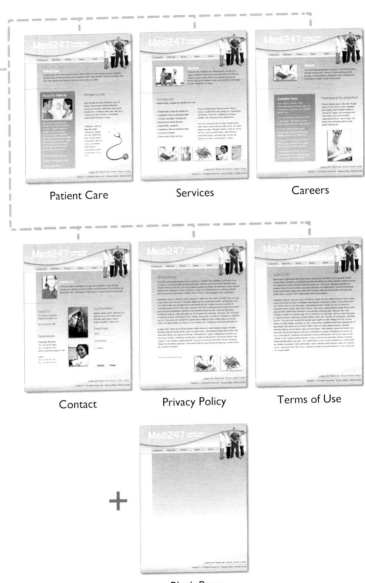

Patient Care

Services

Careers

Contact

Privacy Policy

Terms of Use

+

Blank Page

Pedi-Pooch

Home

Health & Beauty

Training

Pooch Hotel

Contact Us

Privacy Policy

Terms of Use

+

Blank Page

Reptihols

Gallery

💡 For more information on adding Flash photo galleries to your websites, see the *Flash Photo Gallery* tutorial.

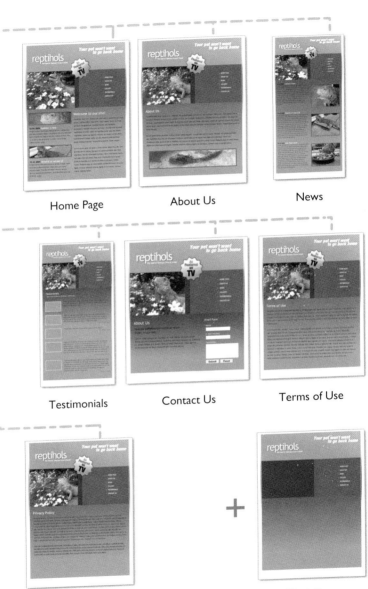

Home Page

About Us

News

Testimonials

Contact Us

Terms of Use

Privacy Policy

+

Blank Page

Urbanwear

Home

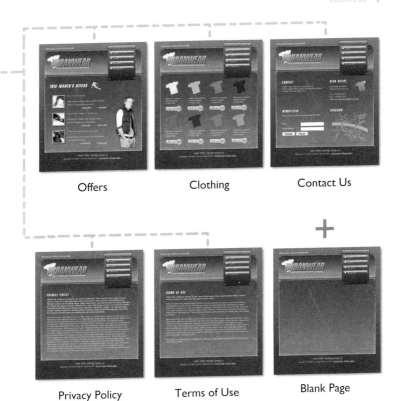

Offers

Clothing

Contact Us

Privacy Policy

Terms of Use

Blank Page

Each template offers three main colour scheme options, but you can also experiment with the other predefined colour schemes, or make your own custom scheme.

At any time during the design process, you can use the **Colour Scheme Designer** to choose a new colour scheme for your site.

For more on colour schemes and the **Colour Scheme Designer**, see online Help and the *Colour Schemes* tutorial.

Megabyte

Contact Us

For information on adding forms to your websites, see *Adding forms* in online Help.

Home

New Products

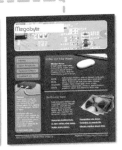

Special Offers

Privacy Policy

Terms of Use

Blank Page

For information on adding e-commerce functionality to your site, see the *E-Commerce* tutorial .

Natro-Med

Main Page

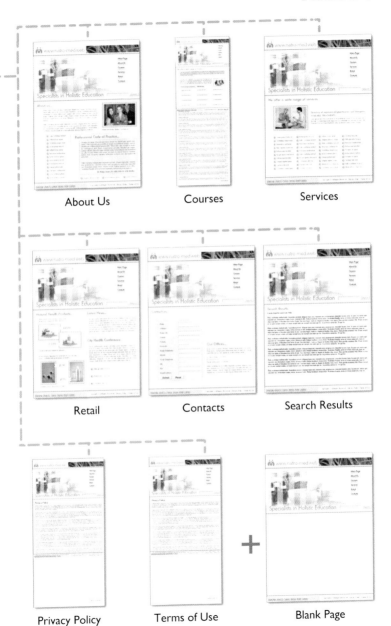

About Us

Courses

Services

Retail

Contacts

Search Results

Privacy Policy

Terms of Use

Blank Page

Teeb Software

Products

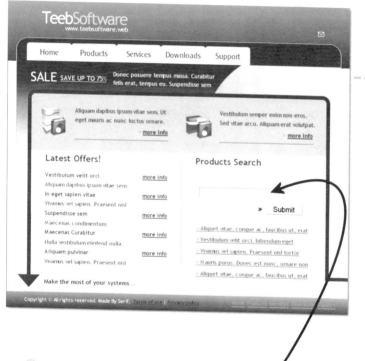

For more information on adding site search functionality, see *Projects: Adding a Search facility* on the **How To** tab.

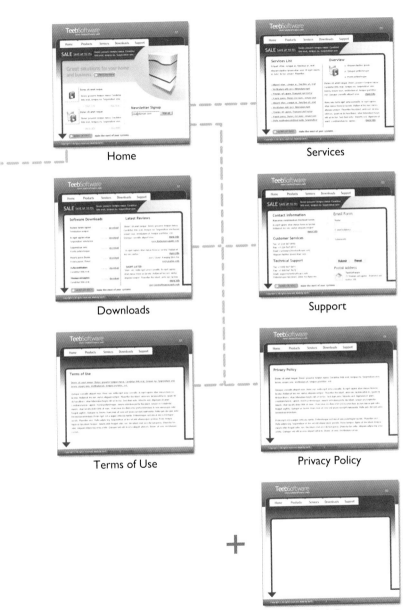

Home

Services

Downloads

Support

Terms of Use

Privacy Policy

+

Blank Page

The Winery House

Home

For more information on adding site search functionality, see *Projects: Adding a Search facility* on the **How To** tab.

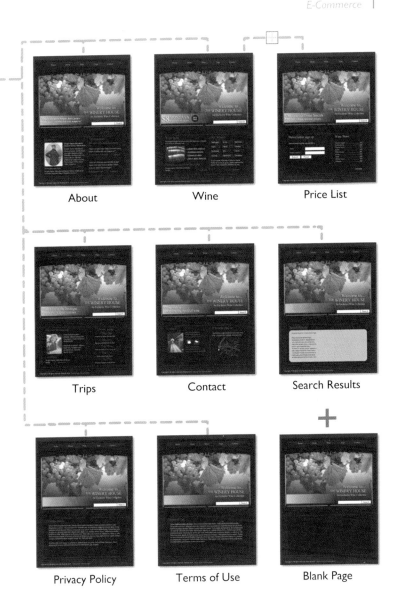

About

Wine

Price List

Trips

Contact

Search Results

Privacy Policy

Terms of Use

Blank Page

Casino

Home

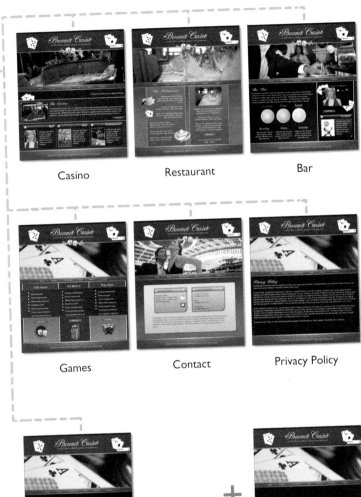

Casino

Restaurant

Bar

Games

Contact

Privacy Policy

Terms of Use

+

Blank Page

Fashion E-Mag

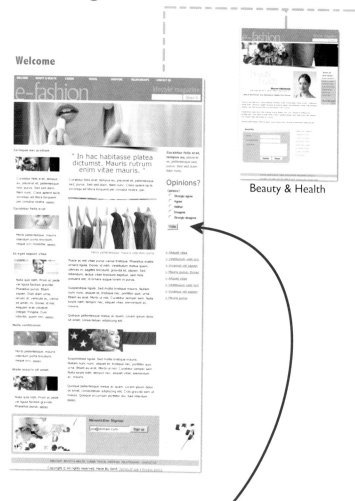

Welcome

Beauty & Health

💡 For more information on adding forms to your websites, see *Adding forms* in online Help.

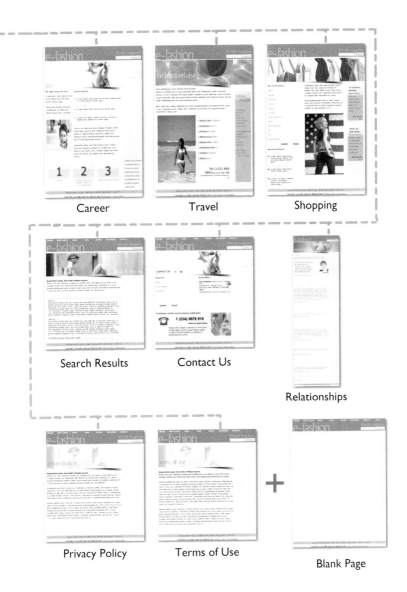

Career

Travel

Shopping

Search Results

Contact Us

Relationships

Privacy Policy

Terms of Use

Blank Page

Our City

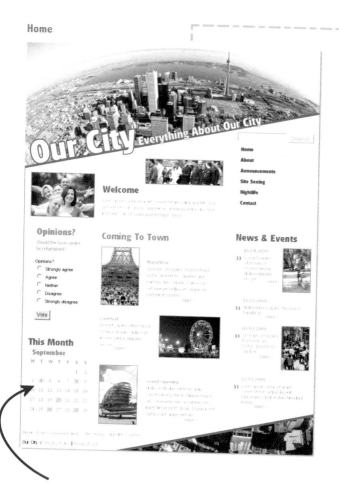

💡 For more information on adding calendars to your websites, see *Adding content: Adding calendars* on the **How To** tab.

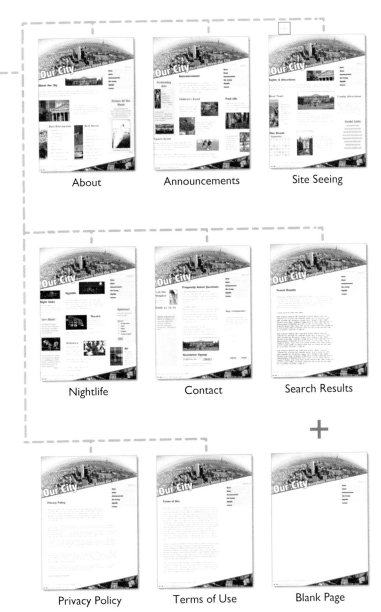

About

Announcements

Site Seeing

Nightlife

Contact

Search Results

Privacy Policy

Terms of Use

Blank Page

Rock Band Blog

Welcome

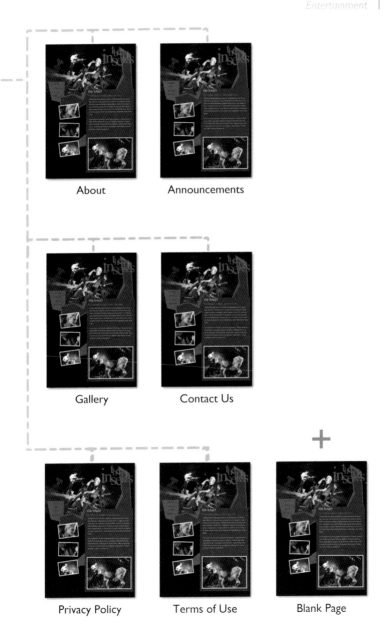

About

Announcements

Gallery

Contact Us

Privacy Policy

Terms of Use

Blank Page

Sushi Sushi

Reviews

Why not add a comment form for your users to leave a review about your product/service or even the site itself?

For information on adding forms to your websites, see *Adding forms* in online Help.

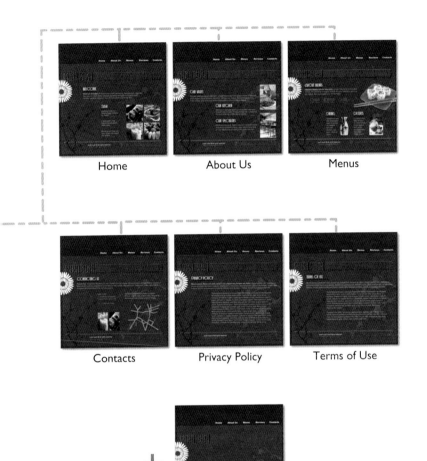

Home

About Us

Menus

Contacts

Privacy Policy

Terms of Use

Blank Page

EasyCook

Home

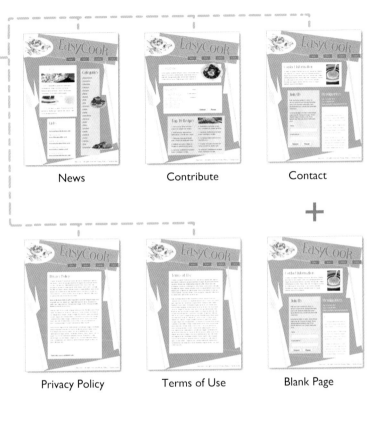

News

Contribute

Contact

Privacy Policy

Terms of Use

Blank Page

At any time during the design process, you can use the **Colour Scheme Designer** to choose a new colour scheme for your site.

Each template offers three colour scheme options, but you can also experiment with the other predefined colour schemes, or make your own custom scheme.

For more information on colour schemes, see the *Colour Schemes* tutorial.

First Impressions

Home

- Home
- About Us
- Get Involved
- Donate
- Contact Us

Welcome...

Maecenas condimentum tincidunt lorem. Vestibulum vel tellus. Sed vulputate. Morbi massa nunc, convallis a, commodo gravida, tincidunt sed, turpis. Aenean ornare viverra est. Maecenas lorem. Aenean euismod lacus dui. Cum sociis natoque penatibus et magnis dis parturient montes, nascetur ridiculus mus. Nulla quam Aenean fermentum, turpis sed

What we do

- Aliquam dapibus ipsum vitae
- Sed vulputate
- Aenean ornare viverra est
- Cum sociis natoque penatibus
- Vestibulum vel tellus
- Aenean ornare viverra
- Nulla quam Aenean
- Maecenas condimentum tincidunt
- Vestibulum vel tellus
- Nulla quam Aenean fermentum

News

14.05.09
Aliquet non, tempus vel, dolor. Integer sapien nibh, egestas ut, cursus sit amet, faucibus a, sapien. Vestibulum purus purus, elementum ac, luctus ullamcorper, ornare vitae, massa. Nullam posuere sem ut mauris. Nullam velit. Quisque sodales. Donec suscipit suscipit erat. Nam blandit. Praesent congue lorem non dolor. Maecenas vitae erat. Ut ac purus vel purus dapibus gravida.

More info

29.04.09
Nullam lorem sapien, tempus ac, fringilla at, elementum sed, purus. Duis molestie pede. Vivamus quis odio sit amet libero sodales tincidunt. Nam sit amet metus vitae lectus ullamcorper dignissim. Suspendisse leo. Praesent justo justo, aliquet ac, accumsan vel, posuere quis, pede. Morbi pretium lacus.

More info

We need you...

Aliquam dapibus ipsum vitae sem. Ut eget mauris ac nunc luctus ornare. Phasellus enim augue, rutrum tempus, blandit in, vehicula eu, neque. Sed consequat nunc. Proin metus. Duis at mi non tellus malesuada tincidunt. Cras in neque. Sed lacinia, felis ut sodales pretium, justo sapien hendrerit est, et convallis nisi quam sit amet erat. Suspendisse consequat nibh a mauris. Curabitur libero ligula, faucibus at, mollis ornare, mattis et, libero.

Aliquam pulvinar congue pede. Fusce condimentum turpis vel dolor. Ut blandit. Sed elementum justo quis sem. Sed eu orci eu ante iaculis accumsan. Sed suscipit dolor quis mi. Curabitur ultrices nonummy lacus. Morbi ipsum ipsum, adipiscing eget, tincidunt vitae, pharetra at, tellus. Nulla gravida, arcu eget dictum elel, velit ligula suscipit nibh, sagittis imperdiet metus nunc non pede. Aenean congue pede in nisi tristique interdum. Sed commodo, ipsum ac dignissim ullamcorper, odio nulla venenatis

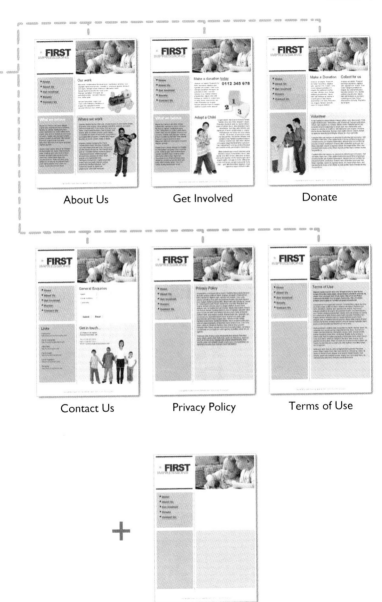

About Us

Get Involved

Donate

Contact Us

Privacy Policy

Terms of Use

+

Blank Page

Green Park

Home

Green Park

| Home | Guide | Events | Contact |

Your refuge from the bustle of daily life

About the Park

Curabitur felis erat, tempus eu placerat et, pellentesque sed, purus. Sed sed diam. Nam nunc. Class aptent taciti sociosqu ad litora torquent per conubia nostra, per. **More**

The History

Nulla quis nibh. Proin ac pede vel ligula facilisis gravida. Phasellus purus. Etiam sapien. Duis diam urna, iaculis ut, vehicula ac, varius sit amet, mi. Donec id nisl. Aliquam erat volutpat. Integer fringilla. Duis lobortis, quam non volutpat. **More**

Visit our Farmyard

Nulla quis nibh. Proin ac pede vel ligula facilisis gravida. Phasellus purus. Etiam sapien. Duis diam urna, iaculis ut, vehicula ac, varius sit amet, mi. Donec id nisl. Aliquam erat volutpat. Integer fringilla. Duis lobortis, quam non volutpat. **More**

Welcome to Green Park!

Curabitur felis erat, tempus eu placerat et, pellentesque sed, purus. Sed sed diam. Nam nunc. Class aptent taciti sociosqu ad litora torquent per conubia nostra, per. Curabitur felis erat, tempus eu placerat et, pellentesque sed, purus. Sed sed diam. Nam nunc. Class aptent taciti sociosqu ad litora torquent per conubia nostra, per. Curabitur felis erat, tempus eu placerat et, pellentesque sed, purus. Sed sed diam. Nam nunc. Class aptent taciti sociosqu ad litora torquent

Morbi pellentesque mauris rhoncus porta.

Should the park be open until 8pm?

Opinions?

Opinions?
- ○ Strongly agree
- ○ Agree
- ○ Neither
- ○ Disagree
- ○ Strongly disagree

Vote

News

Vivamus vel sapien. Praesent nec tortor laoreet eu, dapibus quis, egestas non mauris. Cum sociis natoque penatibus et magnis dis parturient montes, nascetur ridiculus mus. Nullam eleifend pharetra felis. Mauris nibh velit, tristique ac, lacinia in, scelerisque et, ante. Donec viverra tortor sed nulla.

Morbi vel eros dignissim nisi malesuada et convallis quis augue. Vestibulum ante ipsum primis in faucibus orci luctus et ultrices posuere cubilia Curae. Proin aliquam leo ut luctus tempus, eros lectus eleifend massa, quis sollicitudin erat magna non leo. Vestibulum venenatis. Donec sagittis velit sit augue. Fusce in nisl vitae massa venenatis rhoncus. Praesent orci velit, lobortis eget, suscipit semper, congue eu, erat. Quisque malesuada volutpat enim. Vestibulum leo sem, molestie a mattis bibendum feugiat facilisis nisi. Nam scelerisque odio. Suspendisse fermentum faucibus felis. Praesent pharetra, in consequat felis in tellus, in in enim rhoncus ullamcorper, sagittis at placerat eget, mauris. Suspendisse auctor erat at ipsum. Aliquam vitae tortor id massa tincidunt eleifend.

In hac habitasse platea dictumst. Mauris rutrum enim vitae mauris. Proin mattis eleifend pede. Sed pretium ante sit amet elit. Quisque pede tellus, dictum eget, dapibus et, sodales dictum, lectus. Pellentesque in dui molestie sit amet, adipiscing et, arcu quis, arcu. Nulla tellus sem, viverra eu, ultrices ac, mattis et, velit. Maecenas quis magna. Ut viverra nisl eu ipsum. Maecenas rhoncus. Duis mattis hac nec sapien. Nullam eu ante non enim sit amet fringilla. Integer leo. Duis eget enim.

Curabitur felis erat, tempus eu placerat et, pellentesque sed, purus. Sed sed diam. Nam nunc. Class aptent taciti sociosqu ad litora torquent per conubia nostra, per inceptos hymenaeos. Aenean risus est, porttitor vel placerat sit amet, vestibulum sit amet, nibh. Ut faucibus odio quis nisl. Etiam vulputate, sapien eu egestas rutrum, leo neque luctus dolor, sed hendrerit tortor metus ut dui.

Suspendisse ligula. Sed nulla tristique mauris. Nullam nunc nunc, aliquet et, tristique nec, porttitor quis, urna. Etiam eu erat. Morbi ut nisl. Curabitur semper sem. Nulla turpis nibh, tempor nec, aliquet vitae, elementum ac, mauris.

Newsletter Signup

| you@domain.com | Sign up |

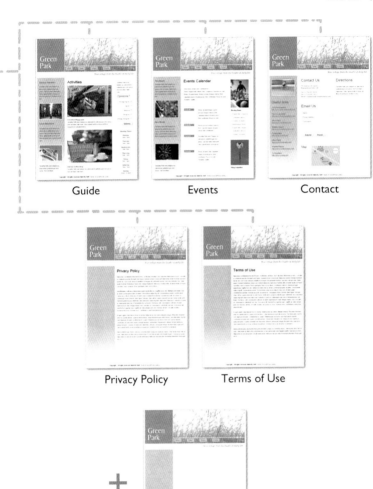

Guide

Events

Contact

Privacy Policy

Terms of Use

Blank Page

Hole In One

Home

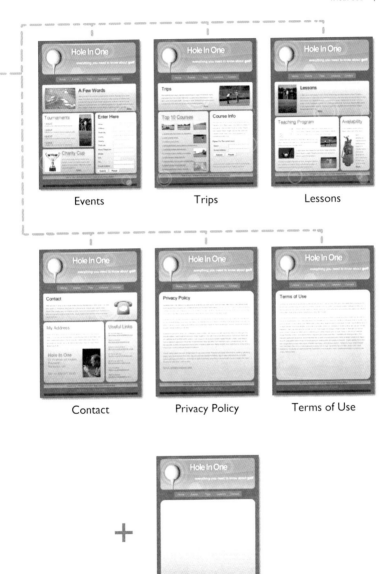

Events

Trips

Lessons

Contact

Privacy Policy

Terms of Use

+

Blank Page

Martial Arts

Classes

💡 You can adopt the functionality used in the templates such as buttons, which take site visitors to another page in your site!

For more information about creating site navigation elements see the tutorial *Navigation Bars*, or the *Setting up navigation* section of the **How To** tab.

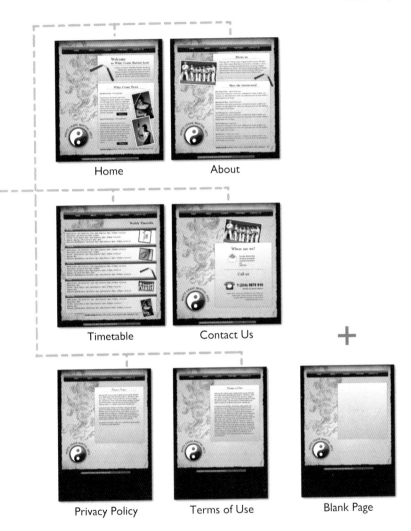

Home

About

Timetable

Contact Us

Privacy Policy

Terms of Use

Blank Page

Reactive

Home

welcome

In hac habitasse platea dictumst. Mauris rutrum enim vitae mauris. Proin mattis eleifend pede. Sed pretium ante sit amet elit. Quisque pede tellus, dictum eget, dapibus ac, sodales dictum, lectus. Pellentesque mi dui, molestie sit amet, adipiscing id, iaculis quis, arcu. Nulla tellus sem, viverra eu, ultricies ac, mattis et, velit. Maecenas quis in hac habitasse platea dictumst. Mauris rutrum enim vitae mauris. Proin mattis eleifend pede. Sed pretium ante sit amet elit. Quisque pede tellus, dictum eget, dapibus ac, sodales dictum, lectus. Pellentesque mi dui, molestie sit amet, adipiscing id, iaculis quis, arcu.

> ### Find your fitness level
> Morbi nisl eros, dignissim nec, malesuada et, convallis quis, augue. Vestibulum ante ipsum. Morbi nisl eros, dignissim nec, malesuada et, convallis quis, augue. Vestibulum ante.

> ### Centres near you
> Morbi nisl eros, dignissim nec, malesuada et, convallis quis, augue. Vestibulum ante ipsum. Morbi nisl eros, dignissim nec, malesuada et, convallis quis, augue.

> ### What makes us different
> Morbi nisl eros, dignissim nec, malesuada et, convallis quis, augue. Vestibulum ante ipsum. Morbi nisl eros, dignissim nec, malesuada et, convallis quis, augue. Vestibulum ante ipsum.

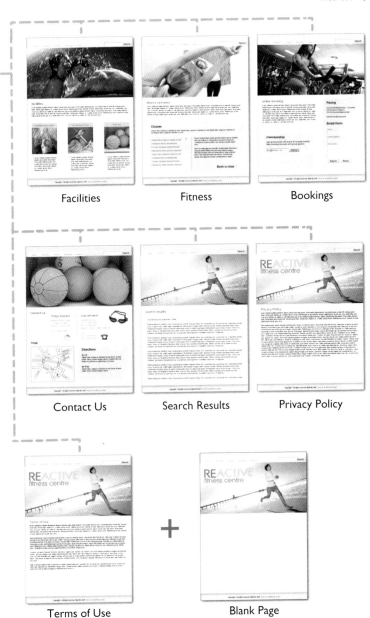

Facilities

Fitness

Bookings

Contact Us

Search Results

Privacy Policy

Terms of Use

Blank Page

Street Level

Welcome

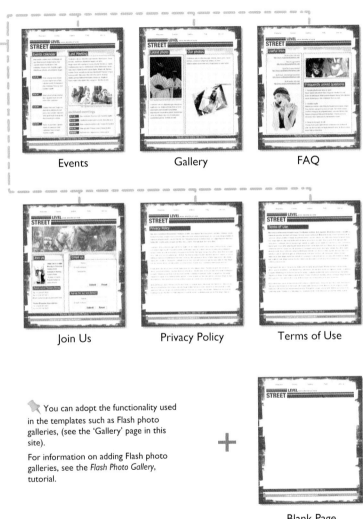

Events

Gallery

FAQ

Join Us

Privacy Policy

Terms of Use

You can adopt the functionality used in the templates such as Flash photo galleries, (see the 'Gallery' page in this site).

For information on adding Flash photo galleries, see the *Flash Photo Gallery*, tutorial.

Blank Page

Sun Hawk Summer Camp

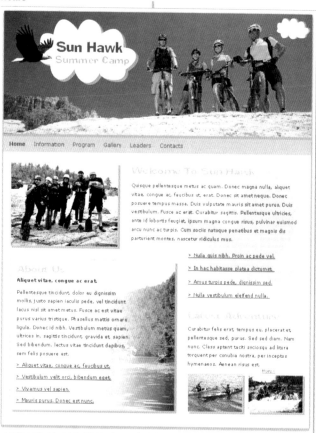

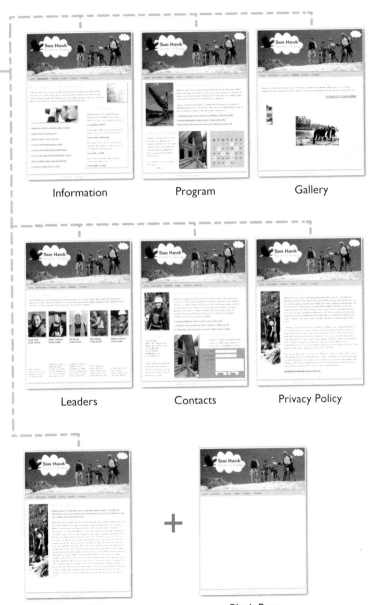

Information

Program

Gallery

Leaders

Contacts

Privacy Policy

Terms of Use

Blank Page

Amelia

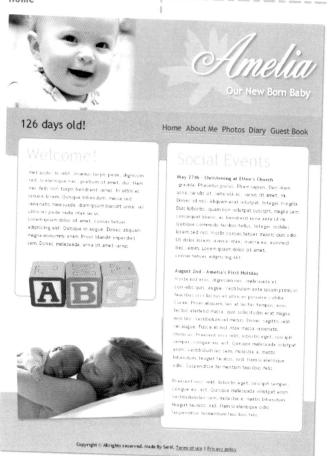

About Me

Photos

Diary

Guest Book

Privacy Policy

Terms of Use

Blank Page

Ceramic Artist

Gallery

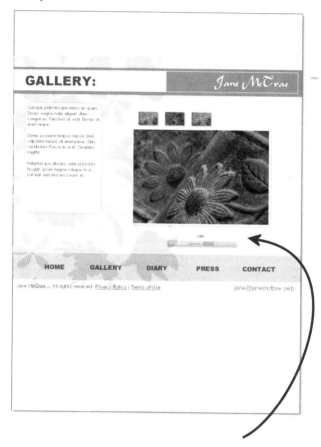

For more information on adding Flash photo galleries to your websites, see the *Flash Photo Gallery* tutorial.

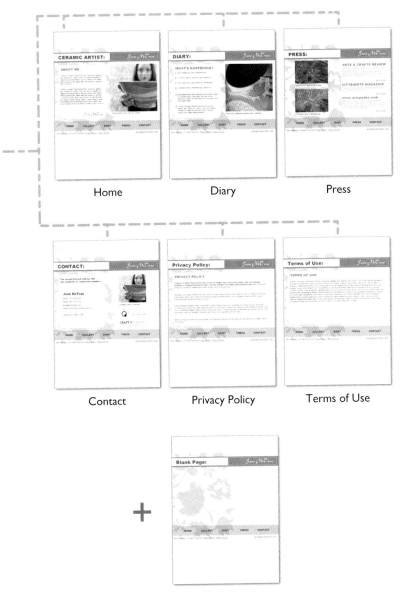

Home

Diary

Press

Contact

Privacy Policy

Terms of Use

+

Blank Page

Holiday Blog

Welcome

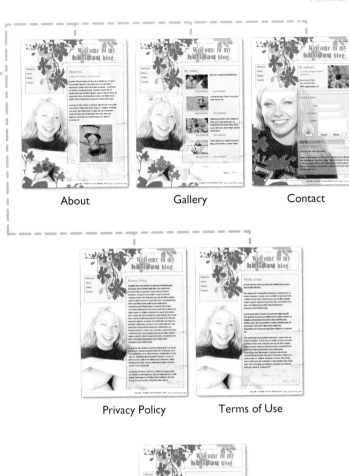

About

Gallery

Contact

Privacy Policy

Terms of Use

Blank Page

Our Baby Boy

Home

Jack Smith

Our Baby Boy

Home   The Run Up   Statistics   Photos

- Birthday
- Christmas
- Baby's First

- Weight
- Likes/Dislikes
- Facts

- Birthday
- Christmas
- Baby's First

www.pregnancytips.web
www.gamesforbaby.web
www.babyshopping.web

Welcome

Donec est nunc, ornare non, aliquet non, tempus vel, dolor. Integer sapien nibh, egestas ut, cursus sit amet, faucibus a, sapien. Vestibulum purus purus, elementum ac, luctus ullamcorper, ornare vitae, massa. Nullam posuere sem ut mauris. Nullam.

Latest News

• 15.08.07
Psum vitae sem. Ut eget mauris ac nunc luctus ornare. Phasellus enim augue, rutrum tempus, blandit in, vehicula eu, hendrerit est et.

• 28.07.07
Suspendisse sem lorem, ornare non, vestibulum ut, tempor porttitor est.

• 02.07.07
Maecenas condimentum tincidunt lorem. Vestibulum vel tellus. Sed vulputate. Morbi massa nunc, convallis a, commodo gravida, tincidunt sed, turpis.

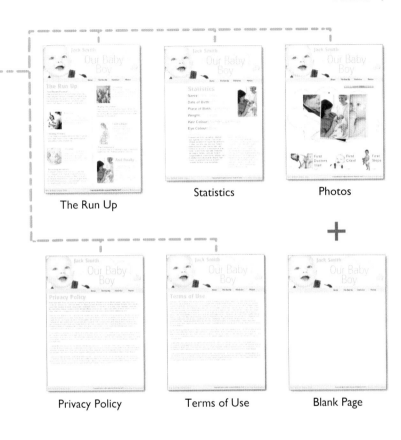

The Run Up

Statistics

Photos

Privacy Policy

Terms of Use

Blank Page

Each template offers three main colour scheme options, but you can also experiment with the other predefined colour schemes, or make your own custom scheme.

At any time during the design process, you can use the **Colour Scheme Designer** to choose a new colour scheme for your site.

For more on colour schemes and the Colour Scheme Designer, see online Help and the *Colour Schemes* tutorial.

Special Day

Home

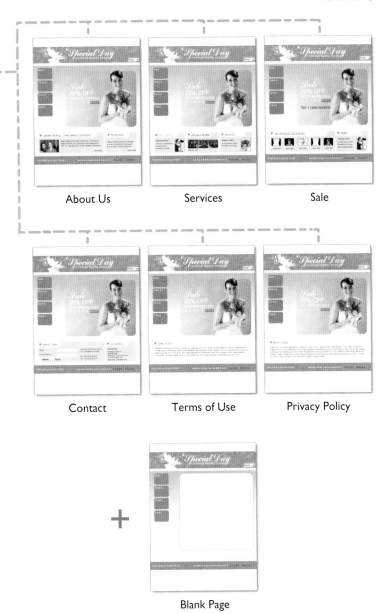

About Us

Services

Sale

Contact

Terms of Use

Privacy Policy

+

Blank Page

T.Reinn

Home

Contact

Privacy Policy

Privacy Policy

 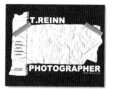

Blank Page

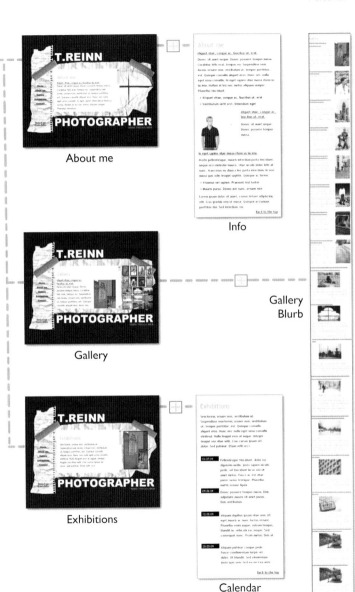

About me

Info

Gallery

Gallery
Blurb

Exhibitions

Calendar

Reactive

Teeb Software

The Winery House

Birthday Invite

Holiday Blog

It's a Boy

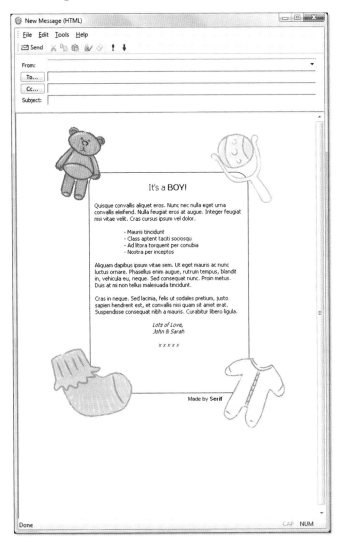

Our Baby

Our Holiday

Picture Frames

Rock Band Blog